Joined-up places?
Social cohesion and neighbourhood regeneration

Ray Forrest and Ade Kearns

In memory of Professor Lindsey Dugdill

1965-2014

UNIVERSITY OF SALFORD

By giving a donation for this book you are honouring Lindsey's memory,
and the money raised will be given to Macmillan

The **Joseph Rowntree Foundation** has supported this project as part of its programme of research and innovative development projects, which it hopes will be of value to policy makers and practitioners. The facts presented and views expressed in this report are, however, those of the authors and not necessarily those of the Foundation.

© Joseph Rowntree Foundation 1999

All rights reserved.

Published by YPS for the Joseph Rowntree Foundation

Cover design by Adkins Design

ISBN 1 902633 33 4

Prepared and printed by:
York Publishing Services Ltd
64 Hallfield Road
Layerthorpe
York YO31 7ZQ

Contents

1	**People and places**	1
	The research	2
	Neighbourhood profiles	3
2	**Aspects of community**	7
	Social cohesion and social capital	7
	Close communities and closed communities	10
	The 'good' neighbourhood	13
	Women in the community	13
	Social cohesion and multiculturalism	16
	Generations and regeneration	19
	Aspects of community: conclusion	22
3	**The neighbourhood environment**	24
	Neighbourhood functions	24
	Community facilities	26
	Social interaction in the neighbourhood	29
	A sense of place and feelings of loss	30
	Big visions and modest projects: community-led environmental improvements	32
	Neighbourhood image and exclusion	33
	The neighbourhood environment: conclusion	36
4	**The experience of regeneration**	38
	Undergoing regeneration	38
	Community involvement and community priorities	38
	Communication and awareness of regeneration	40
	Is professional regeneration needed?	41
	Divided by regeneration	41
	Social regeneration: bringing the community together	42
	(Re)generating optimism and the need for jobs	45
	Regeneration through partnership working	46
	The experience of regeneration: conclusion	47
5	**Conclusions**	49
	Social cohesion	49
	The neighbourhood	50
	Urban regeneration	51
	Neighbourhoods in an urban context	51
	Joined-up places	52
References		53

1 People and places

Does neighbourhood matter? It certainly matters to those with the resources to choose where to live in the city. Reputation and image have strong positive and negative effects on house prices, the costs of private renting and the desirability or otherwise of council estates. And these reputations and images may have broader impacts on employment opportunities, credit rating and more general perceptions of social esteem and social worth. We all have our own personal mental maps of cities which identify the good and the bad neighbourhoods, the gentrifying and the decaying, the safe and the unsafe. Whether or not a neighbourhood can be clearly delineated, the boundaries clearly marked, is not really the issue. To varying extents, we socialise and interact in our local environments and these local environments continue to represent a significant resource in terms of social networks and social identity. However, these local environments are not hermetically sealed but intersect with wider networks. Indeed, it is the quality and degree of interaction with the world beyond the local community which some see as differentiating the integrated from the excluded neighbourhood. Neighbourhoods which contain a high concentration of poor people living in precarious conditions may become increasingly divorced from mainstream society and from the networks which provide access to the world of formal employment. A community may become more defensive and preoccupied with short-term coping and survival strategies. Self-help and mutual aid may be prominent features of such neighbourhoods but survival and cohesion are not incompatible with social exclusion. The former may contribute to the latter.

There is therefore a complicated connection between individuals, groups and places. A recent review of US evidence on neighbourhood effects emphasised that age, gender, income and stage in the life course all affect the influence of neighbourhood. In other words, the neighbourhood matters to some more than others. For those with the least resources, neighbourhood conditions may have the greatest effects. Children, those without work, elderly people are all likely to spend more of their time in and around the home than those in work. The quality of the local school will matter more to those without the resources to buy education elsewhere or to supplement in other ways the education their children receive. Current debate on the nature and extent of social exclusion has tended to focus on the most distressed and disadvantaged neighbourhoods and has once again revived long-standing discussions about the efficacy of place-based as opposed to people-based policies. What is required, however, is a delicate mix of both (Cars *et al*. 1998). Social exclusion arises from a combination of factors which may include unemployment, low income, marital breakdown and a generally resource-poor social network. Whatever the individual combination, it is evident that chronically disadvantaged individuals and households are increasingly trapped within or channelled into specific neighbourhoods. That spatial concentration of poor people is itself an important dimension of social exclusion. In other words, the whole is greater and more complex than the sum of the parts and indicators of individual disadvantage are unable to capture fully the nature of everyday life in those neighbourhoods, the resources which are or could be mobilised and thus the most appropriate policy mix required for regeneration.

The research

Over the last decade, the Joseph Rowntree Foundation has carried out considerable research on disadvantaged neighbourhoods to discover what works in their regeneration. This work has shown, among other things, that each area is different, with its own distinct problems and opportunities. It has also become evident that we knew relatively little about the perceptions, expectations and aspirations of residents themselves or their reactions to regeneration initiatives. As part of the wider JRF Area Regeneration Research Programme, four separate but related research projects were grouped within a mini-programme to pursue these issues. This programme brought together researchers from Teesside, London, Liverpool and Nottingham. All the teams had a strong local knowledge of the areas to be studied and were skilled in qualitative methods. The neighbourhoods varied in terms of size, social composition, physical characteristics and policy histories, but all had clear boundaries and were easily identifiable and recognisable to local people. All four projects were concerned with the physical and social qualities of these neighbourhoods and the interaction between these dimensions. In particular, the research programme was concerned with how poor areas function, the strength and nature of social networks, the extent and nature of formal and informal activity and how residents themselves view their future prospects. In order to explore these issues, the research focused on a number of interrelated components.

- The social glue: Are these cohesive or disorganised communities? What is the nature of the individual and group relationships in which residents participate locally?

- The civic infrastructure: What are the formal organisations and networks functioning locally?

- The physical infrastructure: What is the physical character of the housing and other amenities and the general estate layout? How has it changed through regeneration or decline? What are the focal points for the community?

- The external links: What are the social and spatial links to the world beyond the immediate neighbourhood? To what extent is the neighbourhood socially and spatially isolated?

- The attitudes and expectations of residents: How do residents themselves view their future prospects? How do they feel about their home, their neighbours and the area in general? What is a 'good' neighbourhood? What has been their own experience of regeneration initiatives?

The research was also sensitive to differences of view and expectation within the community in relation to such factors as age, gender and ethnicity. Ideas of a 'good' community for young people may be very different from those held by elderly people. There are communities within communities. And there is community beyond the neighbourhood. That wider community may be differentially experienced by different groups within the neighbourhood and could have a significant impact on priorities and expectations. These issues were taken up in different ways by the research teams in relation to four additional crosscutting themes:

- the views and expectations of younger and older people
- men, women and community
- active and non-active residents
- multiculturalism and community.

It is inappropriate in this summary report to recite endless statistics on poverty and deprivation. Besides, the incantation of such measures conveys little about the life within these neighbourhoods and the views and feelings of the residents which have been the main focus of these studies. The aim has been to bring these places to life, to expose the vibrancy of the relationships within them, to approach them as functioning rather than as dysfunctional areas. As the individual studies have shown, these neighbourhoods are all externally labelled as deprived, disadvantaged and socially excluded areas. They are the kinds of areas which have borne the brunt of economic restructuring and widening income inequalities. But they are not places where residents are in the main passive or dependent. Many residents are actively engaged in a variety of activities. Some are actively engaged in the formal infrastructure of regeneration. Others are more fully occupied in getting by under circumstances of extreme hardship.

This synthesis distils the main findings and lessons for regeneration initiatives from the four separate studies. The more detailed findings can be found in the individual reports which have been published as self-standing documents

(Andersen *et al.*, 1999; Cattell and Evans, 1999; Silburn *et al.*, 1999; Wood and Vamplew, 1999).

Neighbourhood profiles

The boxed profiles below provide a general summary of the key features of the eight study neighbourhoods. Taken together, they contain all the usual ingredients of decline and disadvantage. They are places where the economic base which originally sustained them has collapsed or substantially contracted. In some cases, this has been of relatively recent origin. In others, the local job market has a long history of precariousness and contraction. Dwelling conditions are generally below average associated with unimproved, older dwellings or with the less popular locations and designs of post-war council housing. In the inner city areas, there is the familiar picture of low quality private renting with overcrowding and lack of amenities.

All the areas are disadvantaged according to the conventional indicators of unemployment, poverty and deprivation but there is substantial variation in relation to physical appearance, location within their respective urban areas, the impact of past regeneration initiatives and social composition. All the areas suffer from long-standing stigma and negative reputations. They are the kinds of neighbourhoods which are in the minds of politicians, the media and the general population when discussion turns to social exclusion. Youth unemployment is generally high, property values are relatively low, in some cases there are abandoned and empty dwellings, council vacancies are less sought after than in other areas, crime is higher than average, there are high proportions of

Joined-up places?

children eligible for free school meals and relatively high levels of lone parenthood.

In some cases, and this is a major differentiating feature, they are places where the retail and other community facilities are either non-existent or low quality. The shops, the banks, the post office have gone elsewhere leaving residents dependent on more distant and inevitably more expensive options. In some of the inner city neighbourhoods, however, low income, bad housing conditions and other indicators of deprivation and disadvantage co-exist with local shops and facilities to create a very different set of day-to-day experiences for residents. They could all be described as mixed tenure areas but for highly varied reasons. While the majority of the neighbourhoods are mainly council built estates with varying levels of home ownership via the Right to Buy, others such as Hyson Green and Forest Fields in Nottingham are more typical inner city areas with a legacy of older nineteenth-century terraces combined with different phases of clearance and redevelopment. Whereas the East London estates of Kier Hardie and Trowbridge have over 60 per cent of residents in the council sector, in Forest Fields around 7 per cent of residents are in that tenure. In their local contexts, all have relatively low levels of home ownership, but levels of owner occupation vary from over 50 per cent in Forest Fields to less than 30 per cent in the Liverpool and London neighbourhoods.

All the areas are and have been the subject of regeneration initiatives over the years. The redevelopment and refurbishment have in some cases been substantial in terms of both the scale of investment and the visible change to the housing stock and estate layout. However, despite the substantial energies and funds which have come from outside and the activities of local groups and individuals, the basic indicators of disadvantage have in the main stayed relatively unchanged. While in some neighbourhoods trajectories of decline may have levelled out and indeed some greater optimism may have been generated for the future, the external images of these neighbourhoods remains highly negative. Tenure diversification beyond the Right to Buy, demolition and build for sale, changes to the physical condition and layout of dwellings and infrastructure and new enclaves of owner occupation have had little impact on the underlying processes of disadvantage and exclusion.

Trowbridge, Hackney Wick, Hackney
- Inner city estate.
- Very high levels of poverty and unemployment.
- Mainly council built and owned.
- A 1990s' development of terraces, squares and low rise flats replacing original 1960s' towers (Wick Village). Bungalows and low rise flats in the remaining part of the estate with adjacent mixed tenure development.
- Few shops and virtually no other facilities.
- Physically isolated.
- Ethnically mixed but higher proportion of white households than borough average.
- Relatively high proportions of elderly people and under 18s.
- Subject to extensive redevelopment since the mid-1960s.

People and places

Forest Fields, Nottingham
- Inner city neighbourhoods, about a mile north of the city centre.
- Predominantly late Victorian and Edwardian terraced housing, some still lacking basic amenities.
- High population density.
- Mixed tenure but mainly owner occupied and substantial private renting.
- Mainly residential with some local shops.
- Ethnically mixed, with high concentration of Pakistani and Indian households.

St Hilda's, Middlesbrough
- Inner city but in isolated location.
- Few local shops, no local schools.
- Long history of decline and stigma.
- Substantial population decline.
- Mainly council housing with low quality private renting and home ownership with problems of resale and negative equity.
- Increasing numbers of empty dwellings.
- Substantial clearance activity in mid-1950s with replacement by mainly council flats and maisonettes; 1980s' clearance of 1950s' flats replaced with owner occupied and housing association houses.

Dingle, Liverpool
- Mixed tenure, inner city.
- Almost half council owned.
- Population decline associated with clearance and local job losses.
- Relatively busy throughway with good connections to city centre.
- Very low levels of car ownership.
- Local shopping area with supermarket, local schools and other recreational and community facilities.
- Substantial recent clearance activity with replacement of old terraces/tenements with smaller clusters of houses in co-ops or small estates.
- ERDF (European Regional Development Fund) funded Pathways Partnership with SRB (Single Regeneration Budget) status.

Hyson Green, Nottingham
- Mixed housing pattern with history of redevelopment.
- A busy throughway to the city centre.
- High population density.
- Mixed tenure with roughly equal owner occupied, private renting and council housing.
- Mix of retail and commercial activities in decline.
- Ethnically mixed, around a fifth of residents from the Indian sub-continent and Caribbean.

Keir Hardie estate, Canning Town, Newham
- Inner city estate.
- Very high levels of poverty and unemployment.
- Very high proportion of lone parent households.
- Few shops and virtually no other amenities.
- Mainly council built in different post-war phases; mix of tower blocks, low rise and terraces.
- Relatively high proportions of elderly people and under 18s.
- Physically isolated.
- Higher proportion of white households than borough average but ethnic mix increasing.

Joined-up places?

Norton Grange, Stockton-on-Tees
- Outer city estate of mainly semi-detached and terraced housing.
- No local shops or schools.
- Relatively high levels of lone parenthood, unemployment and low skilled work.
- Originally 1930s-built council housing as part of slum clearance drive.
- Mixed tenure with roughly equal mix of housing association, council housing and home ownership.
- Extensive modernisation in 1970s.
- Some demolition in early 1980s with replacement by some low rise council and housing association properties for elderly people.
- Major revitalisation in 1990s funded by City Challenge with clearance of half the estate.

Speke, Liverpool
- Large, physically isolated, self-contained, outer city estate.
- Majority tenure council housing–recently transferred to housing association.
- Declining infrastructure associated with local factory closures since the 1970s.
- Major population losses since early 1970s.
- Limited shopping and other amenities.
- Inadequate public transport combined with low levels of car ownership.
- Currently ERDF funded Pathways Partnership with SRB status.

2 Aspects of community

Social cohesion and social capital

Social cohesion is a central theme in both the JRF (Joseph Rowntree Foundation) Area Regeneration and ESRC (Economic and Social Research Council) Cities Programmes. Both programmes are interested in the idea of social cohesion as a necessary quality of the well functioning city or neighbourhood, and in the policies which may be required to enhance and encourage cohesion. It is also widely assumed that many of the problems associated with disadvantaged areas reflect and exacerbate a lack of social cohesion. Indeed, there is a more general view that we live in a world where social cohesion is under threat from changing employment opportunities, the impact of new technology, the erosion of the traditional family form, widening social divisions and a progressive erosion of the formal and informal institutions which have apparently bound us together for much of this century. The idea that major social and economic forces are at work undermining the essential social fabric is, of course, by no means novel. At the turn of the last century, social commentators were preoccupied with the corrosive and transformative impacts of urbanisation and urbanism on the traditional ties of community. A social order where work and home were closely integrated, space was shared, kinship links were close and there were common religious and moral values was being replaced by one in which processes of competition, anonymity and individualism prevailed and where social stability was more precarious. Social cohesion, the social glue of a society, therefore has a number of dimensions and can be addressed at a number of levels. The literature on this is diverse (for a general overview, see Kearns and Forrest, 1998, paper presented to the Social Policy Association Conference, University of Lincolnshire and Humberside, 14–16 July) but encompasses ideas of:

- a shared sense of belonging or common purpose

- social solidarity between groups and across generations

- shared values and beliefs minimising conflict and allowing for social stability

- active, well intentioned citizens

- dense networks of friends, family or acquaintances

- a positive and sentimental attachment to local traditions, institutions and places.

In current debates on this issue, the residential neighbourhood remains central but as a source of disagreement regarding its continuing relevance in the shaping of our social identities and life chances and its relative importance in maintaining the social glue of contemporary urban society. There are a number of aspects to this debate. The dominant view is that the fluidity of contemporary life in terms of spatial mobility and social relationships has meant that we are less rooted in particular cities or parts of cities than in the past. The neighbourhood represents only part of an increasingly diverse web of relationships of kin, friends, colleagues and other contacts which may be citywide, national or international. These relationships may be routine, occasional, face to face, or remote and virtual via e-mail and

Joined-up places?

the world wide web. These contacts and links are our portfolio of resources which shape our everyday lives and multiple identities. But these networks are more than simply routes to opportunities or material resources. The nature and quality of these networks affect how we see ourselves and others, the values we hold and the general quality of lives we lead. The residential neighbourhood may therefore be of greater significance to some groups than others. Moreover, there are some (for example, Henning and Lieberg, 1996) who point to the importance of the casual contacts of neighbouring and the 'weak' ties of residence in providing bridges to the world outside and in providing a sense of worth and identity. From this perspective, daily interactions in and around the home remain significant building blocks in the creation of the social glue. Cohesion is essentially bottom-up rather than top-down.

Whilst it is difficult to specify or measure with any precision the degree and nature of social cohesion at societal, city or neighbourhood level, it is generally held that widening inequalities, rising poverty and social division will act against greater social stability and solidarity. This is most explicitly expressed in the context of the European Union. The *First Report on Economic and Social Cohesion* (European Commission, 1996) pointed to the reduction of inequalities in living conditions and employment opportunities as prerequisites for a Europe of cohesive, active citizens with a sense of common purpose and belonging. Pockets of chronic poverty and disadvantage are recognised as pervasive and visible barriers to achieving the social aspirations of the European Union. At the pan-European level, therefore, the local neighbourhood has been an important focus for initiatives and funding – a cohesive Europe to be built as much from the bottom up as from the well intentioned but remote rhetoric at the top.

We have moved some way from long-standing debates about whether policy should focus on disadvantaged people, or places where disadvantaged people are concentrated. It is recognised that neighbourhoods are relational webs rather than simply aggregations of individuals or families with a variety of disadvantages. Herein lies their importance. Places are not excluded but the poor, via a variety of routes and circumstances, are channelled into parts of cities characterised by low quality environments, negative images and networks which are resource weak. The preoccupation of everyday life in these neighbourhoods is dominated by getting by. Those who can, get out, further weakening the social and physical infrastructure. Healey (1998) emphasises this shift in emphasis from merely focusing on the quality of housing provision in such areas to seeing neighbourhoods as 'social worlds which shape attitudes and aspirations'. The critical feature of areas of chronic disadvantage is that in these places 'attitudes and aspirations may be significantly different from those people who live in other parts of the city and may be internally differentiated as well'. The internal dynamics of such areas is an important dimension of social exclusion with the implication that 'some neighbourhoods are drifting away from the norms of society as a whole' (Healey, 1998, p. 54). The relative importance of the neighbourhood in people's lives is therefore an aspect of wider social polarisation. But it is a polarisation or contrast which has more than one dimension. The 'successful' suburb may have few of the features of community or neighbourliness (Baumgartner, 1988) but will contain people with rich and diverse relational webs. Conversely, the poor neighbourhood may have weak and inward-looking networks which nevertheless offer strong support in adversity. The very strength and introverted nature of these networks may be a disadvantaging factor. Social cohesion and social exclusion are not necessarily opposites, neither are poverty and disorganisation. The internally cohesive neighbourhood may conjure up romanticised images of community lost or of settled, comfortable villages with a diverse but integrated mix of people, activities and facilities. But there can be cohesive communities in conflict. The cohesive neighbourhood may be in conflict with the wider urban area in which it sits. There is the cohesion of vigilantism or street gangs.

In a slightly different context, it is some of these features of poor neighbourhoods which Portes and Landolt (1996) refer to as the 'downside of social capital'. Social capital incorporates ideas of social networks but as part of broader patterns and qualities of civic engagement. 'By analogy to physical capital and human capital, social capital refers to the norms and networks of civil society that lubricate cooperative action among both citizens and their institutions. Without adequate supplies of social capital – that is, without civic engagement, healthy community institutions, norms of mutual reciprocity, and trust – social institutions falter' (Putnam, 1998). Putnam has argued elsewhere that there is a decline in the stock of social capital in contemporary USA and that poor neighbourhoods in general lack the necessary qualities of self-help, mutuality and trust which could assist in their generation – and in part explain, and are a cumulative product of, their decline (Putnam, 1993, 1996). These ideas have now entered the policy and political arena in Britain. Regeneration strategies have increasingly come to be seen as working with and building on the stock of social capital in a neighbourhood. A key implication is that, without sufficient social capital, regeneration policies will not take root or be sustainable. Neighbourhoods where existing relations of trust and reciprocity are weak will lack the qualities which can create and sustain voluntary association and partnership.

This is inevitably a contentious area. The concept of social capital itself is not without problems and like any concept tends to lose precision with increasing use in a variety of contexts. And there is a basic difficulty in arguing that poor neighbourhoods lack social capital when many studies show contrary evidence. Close family ties, mutual aid and voluntarism are often strong features of poor areas. It is these qualities which may enable people to cope with poverty, unemployment and wider processes of social exclusion. Portes and Landolt (1996) point out that 'There is considerable social capital in ghetto areas, but the assets obtainable through it seldom allow participants to rise above their poverty' (p. 20). Moreover, close social ties can create 'downward-levelling pressures' with pressures to conform to a set of norms and values which make it difficult for individuals to enter mainstream society. 'The same kinds of ties that sometimes yield public goods also produce "public bads": mafia families, prostitution rings, and youth gangs, to cite a few' (Portes and

Landolt, p. 20). In other words, the social relations in a neighbourhood cannot be separated from the social context in which they operate. A high degree of mutual and voluntary activity in a neighbourhood lacking key economic resources of jobs and incomes will produce quite different outcomes and be the product of very different pressures compared with similarly observed activities in an affluent area.

Close communities and closed communities

There is a substantial literature on the internal dynamics of inner city and disadvantaged neighbourhoods. Suttles (1972) talks in terms of the 'defended neighbourhood' when he refers particularly to neighbourhoods under threat, characterised by a population with limited power and resources. Feelings of belonging and territoriality may be generated in different ways. It may come through single issue campaigns which bring people together to resist the closure of a school or other significant community amenity. It may be the territoriality of street gangs with their own code of conduct and strong sense of 'turf' ownership. There may be a longer-standing protest or campaign against the plans of developers or the local authority. The day-to-day activity of getting by in a poor area may contribute to feelings of neighbourliness and belonging to a particular part of the city. Suttles goes to great pains to emphasise that the process of defence generally calls for 'concerted action' of some kind. However short-lived, that coming together of people will tend to 'produce at least traces of cohesion that endure for purposes other than defense' (pp. 34–5). Alliances and boundaries will shift and there may be uneasy tensions between the defence of the neighbourhood and other ties of kin or ethnicity. Nonetheless, the implication is that resistance contributes to the social capital of a neighbourhood through collective endeavour, mutual aid and community activities. Trust and tolerance are generated through collective action.

Diversity and similarity in terms of age, ethnicity or social class are also important factors in neighbourhood stability. Hirschfield and Bowers' (1997) exploration of social cohesion in Liverpool, for example, tends to suggest that the greater the social heterogeneity of an area the more disorganised it will be in terms of informal social controls. The implication is that crime rates will tend to be higher in more socially and ethnically mixed inner city areas. They also draw on the research of US sociologists such as Kasarda and Janowitz (1974) and Sampson (1988) which points to mobility and turnover as perhaps the overriding critical element. Feelings of belonging, community activity, social ties and social networks will all be stronger in areas with a relatively stable population. Stability can of course be the product of entrapment and poverty rather than satisfaction, choice and affluence. Population turnover comes in various forms and for different reasons. And, as we have already commented upon earlier, close ties can have negative dimensions and be disabling if they are exclusionary, inward-looking and divisive.

Our eight neighbourhoods in varying ways contain both positive and negative features of closeness and neighbourliness. Some contain a high diversity of ethnic groups. Some contain

Aspects of community

enclaves of close kin and long-established neighbours. All have experienced some degree of population change and turnover, and this is seen generally as tending to undermine trust and familiarity. Divisions within the areas are often expressed in terms of locals and newcomers or insiders and outsiders. In the London study, on Trowbridge/Wick, there is a long-standing division which relates to the different routes into the area. One group was rehoused from the original tower blocks when they were demolished. Others were allocated as homeless or moved from other estates. Those from outside the original estate are viewed as beneficiaries of regeneration campaigns fought for by those from the tower blocks. Newcomers are often associated with less popular parts or newer parts of an estate, the areas of higher turnover, and blamed for its perceived decline. Older, more established residents contrast their own family histories and patterns of parenting with the newer, younger families who seem to lack the parental control of previous generations. In this sense, the perceived divisions between local people and newcomers may be more a reflection of age and generational differences, of differences of lifestyle and attitude rather than necessarily length of residence. Nevertheless, the close-knit nature of one section of a community, the strong community within a neighbourhood, can act to further disadvantage those moving in:

> *It is difficult sometimes for newcomers – including the formerly homeless, refugees, and single parents – to be accepted in an area [like Canning Town] where 'looking after your own' is a core traditional value.* (Cattell and Evans, 1999)

Newcomers, particularly if they are perceived to be better off than older residents and if they lack any local connections, are also more likely to be the victims of crime and harassment. This was particularly evident from the Teesside work in St Hilda's where informal rules operated in relation to criminal activity and the reporting of crime:

> *The most vulnerable are those who are seen as outsiders, on the fringe of the community, those who perhaps do not share the same values and understanding with regard to crime, often recent arrivals who have no idea of the rules of the game or will not accept them. Another disadvantage of being a new arrival is a lack of knowledge of who the potential wrongdoers are and therefore who to be on guard against.*
> (Wood and Vamplew, 1999)

These informal rules also operated in relation to 'grassing' – which was generally seen as unacceptable – and locally sanctioned crime. While theft from businesses, cars and shoplifting might be seen as acceptable coping strategies, thieving from locals, the community centre or the local school was not.

There were therefore communities within communities with more established residents tending to view population turnover as a factor which undermined trust, tolerance and familiarity. 'Community' had been eroded through population churning and the exodus of those seeking work and more attractive living environments. There is therefore a highly uneven pattern of networking and neighbouring which can vary from street to street. In some parts of an estate or neighbourhood, social bonds are deeply entrenched with close kin living nearby and neighbours of long standing. In other areas,

Joined-up places?

particularly where there is high turnover, contacts are weak and transitory. These features can be especially evident in areas with a diverse ethnic mix. For example, in the Hyson Green and Forest Fields neighbourhoods in Nottingham, the social infrastructure and cultural norms of the Asian community produce a dense network of social ties and contacts. While these bonds become stronger as people become more established through length of residence and chain migration, in other areas, quite contrary processes are at work:

> We never get to know each other because they're never here long enough. I mean you'll get a family, around the corner somewhere, you see them regularly, say, start with hello and then it's a cup of coffee or a night out whatever, within four months they're gone, they're just gone and then it starts all over again, another lot come in and it's like a treadmill, it just goes on and on.
> (Local resident, Nottingham)

It is difficult in these circumstances to build up trust and feelings of commonality and belonging. High turnover in poor neighbourhoods breeds suspicion and accentuates difference. This is particularly marked where some newcomers are associated with anti-social behaviour creating a more generally defensive reaction among neighbours. There are clearly tensions in some of the neighbourhoods where there are older, established enclaves where people look back to a time when the area was more settled and there were jobs. They have experienced a long history of decline and disappointment, and associate the influx of new residents with different outlooks and lifestyles as symptomatic of a downward spiral. Hard drugs, verbal and physical abuse may have come with some of the new residents and these kinds of tensions are understandable. However, the evident tensions expressed in terms of outsiders and locals or references to newcomers may reflect the more general frictions of population churning. These are typically the types of neighbourhoods where too many people simply pass through on their way from one precarious set of circumstances to another. They are not there long enough for trust and familiarity to develop. Population turnover is a normal feature of all neighbourhoods. Even disproportionately high turnover may be of little importance in an area where residents have jobs and money. In that context, it may simply mean that neighbours rarely meet and relations are merely amicable and short lived. Baumgartner (1988) has conjured up this image of the disinterested anonymity of the suburbs where the social capital of trust and mutuality is little in evidence. Local social networks extend narrowly into the world beyond with limited social investment in the residential neighbourhood. In disadvantaged areas, however, where there has been a major depletion of real material resources, population churning has a more serious corrosive impact on the capacity of local residents to sustain commitment to regeneration and optimism for the future:

> You're safe with your kids to play out and things like that, you know everyone and everyone's dead nice, you can run next door, borrow your cup of sugar or whatever, everyone helps each other, and, if anyone had a crisis on their hands, everyone would rally round to help them, things like that. (Resident of St Hilda's, Teesside)

Aspects of community

It's all down to the people ... We've got a brilliant community. (Resident of Speke)

All the studies emphasise resilience in the face of adversity, widespread commitment to community activities, the importance of mutual aid and neighbourhood support networks, and a belief that if anything is going to be achieved it is up to the residents themselves. There is also, however, a strong sense of frustration and disappointment at the failings of past initiatives which have contributed in many cases to a decline in community activity and involvement. This frustration, as discussed later, is partly directed at the experts who come in with their policies and solutions which don't work leaving the residents to pick up the pieces. And there is a sapping of the spirit when despite the rhetoric and the resources nothing much is seen to have changed. 'It's been going on for years now, and people just sit back and say, "yeah, I'll believe it when I see it"' (Andersen *et al.*, 1999). Overall, feelings among many were also nicely encapsulated by a resident of Speke who referred to there being 'Too many organisations and not enough shops'.

The 'good' neighbourhood

Brower's (1996) pursuit of the idea of the good neighbourhood in the US context shows a diversity of ideals and aspirations. As he says, 'Ask people to describe a good neighbourhood, and what you get if you add it up is a place with one door on Fifth Avenue, another on a New England common, and a window looking out to the mountains' (p. 1). The residents in our neighbourhoods have less exotic aspirations and there is a remarkable level of consistency across generations, gender and areas as to the necessary qualities of the good neighbourhood. Good neighbourhoods have good neighbours. It is about people rather than place. This inevitably reflects the run down and unattractive nature of much of the physical environment which people experience on a daily basis. While the quality of the neighbourhood as a physical entity might be condemned, the qualities of 'community', of the people living in the area, were often fiercely defended.

Focus group discussions and individual interviews emphasised a variety of aspects of the good, cohesive neighbourhood or community:

- caring for one another
- being known and knowing everyone
- friendly and helpful
- well behaved and disciplined children
- a place to have fun and social events
- a safe, secure environment
- a core of long-standing residents.

But a good neighbourhood also needs access to jobs, good transport links and basic amenities. There is also a tension between those who seek diversity and difference as the essential ingredients of a vibrant community, and a view of cohesion and community which emphasises similarities of life stage, attitudes and circumstances: 'A solidarity which embraces inter-group cooperation and respect for difference is not always what people have in mind' (Cattell and Evans, 1999).

Women in the community

Suttles (1972) observed that 'Next to children, mothers with young children are probably the most confined and involved in the defended neighbourhood. At minimum they have an interest in knowing enough of the neighbourhood to advise and direct the movement and associations of their children' (p. 40). Previous work for the Joseph Rowntree Foundation on area regeneration has also highlighted the critical role played by women in community life and the contrasts between the genders in terms of activism and informal care. McCulloch (1997), for example, concluded that 'Community work is largely performed by women in their own areas because they are, through tradition and circumstance, committed to them'. He goes on to suggest that 'Mothering is the paradigmatic example of generalised reciprocity and it is women in their early thirties with children who constitute one of the major groups of activists' (p. 66).

These kinds of views resonate with all the studies in the mini-programme. Women experience disadvantage in different ways from men and are generally more actively concerned with facilities for children and child care. The quality and location of schools affects their lives more directly and the 'school gate' is a focal point for discussion:

Women in Speke had organised themselves and successfully campaigned for a health centre, rooted in shared experience of the lack of local services for their children and developed from school gate discussions about the problems this caused them. (Andersen et al., 1999)

Moreover:

...the tasks involved in running the home, looking after children and caring for other adults bring women into more contact than men with statutory agencies such as schools, health and social services on behalf of the people they are looking after. (Andersen et al., 1999)

Women of all ages play a critical role in maintaining the social fabric of the neighbourhoods and in being actively engaged in the formal and informal organisations. These are areas with often relatively high proportions of dependent children, lone mothers and elderly women. Also, the gender composition of the neighbourhoods has changed over time as job losses in traditional male sectors have contributed to an exodus of men. Cultural norms among different ethnic groups do, however, affect the role of women in different community activities. In the ethnically mixed areas of Hyson Green and Forest Fields in Nottingham, for example, Pakistani women tend to be less active in the public sphere:

It is not yet culturally normal for Pakistani married women to take an active part in public life outside the home, and so, unlike their white counterparts, they do not play a prominent part in local residents' groups or other voluntary groups in the neighbourhood. (Silburn et al., 1999)

Social networks pivot around children in relation to schooling, child care and general concerns about safety and security. Moreover, while women's involvement in community organisations and campaigns can be associated with their traditional roles and responsibilities in bringing up children, the social role of men in a deprived community has become more complicated. The loss of position as the principal breadwinner may induce apathy and indifference, and be reflected in a lack of commitment to the day-to-day running of voluntary and community organisations:

Aspects of community

They've got no role, no place, there's nothing that they can do, there are no jobs and if they've got money then they're the odd one out and they can get into drinking or drugs ... You can't seem to get them involved with the kids, even to get little football teams going or anything like that, you can't. When we were young there were boxing clubs and the football and all that, they have nothing now. (Andersen et al., 1999)

When unemployment is pervasive, men who are in work may feel uncomfortable in relation to friends and neighbours who are unemployed. And, over time, as more men leave the area, the gender composition of a street or block may change as lone parent families are allocated to the properties vacated. A middle aged man in the Kier Hardie estate in London commented on his peculiar situation as both male and employed:

In this block of eight maisonettes, I'm the only one who goes to work. The rest are mainly single parents. When there are problems round here – like drunks on the swings at night – they all wait for me to do something about it. When we first lived round here, there were lots of men. We didn't have any bother then, because they'd all come out to sort out any trouble.
(Cattell and Evans, 1999)

For both men and women, however, involvement in community activities requires both time and energy. Other claims on time, the daily grind of simply getting by and the energy expended on looking after children all contribute to inactivity in wider community commitments. There may also be a lack of self-confidence among many regarding public meetings and engaging with officialdom. While women, particularly those with young children, may be more directly concerned, and more directly affected by the lack of local shops and facilities, running the house and feeding the family produce many competing pressures. If women want to attend meetings and get actively involved, they will probably have to bring their children with them. The lack of crèche and after school facilities is a major problem as regards taking on paid work, and also means that friends and neighbours have to be relied upon as childminders: 'They want women to go back to work but how can a woman go back to work without a crèche or after-school facilities'? (Andersen *et al.*, 1999). Assistance targeted at young mothers to encourage registration on training schemes excludes those aged 25 and over and child care expenses are payable only to registered childminders. These eligibility rules, whether justified or not, operate to inhibit women in seeking work and limit the resources which can flow into the neighbourhood through child care activities.

It is also women who have to cope most with the problems of making ends meet in areas where shops have disappeared and where there is little choice. Local shops may be better geared to local incomes and needs but limited in range. Buying children's clothes and shoes will normally necessitate a trip to town. This may involve inadequate public transport and the expense of a more distant shopping trip. With limited financial resources, mothers have to cope with the costs of getting there combined with the inevitable demand from their children for treats:

Joined-up places?

If you want to buy shoes for your kids you've got to drag them into town ... and they start playing up as soon as you get there ... McDonald's, that's the first thing they say ... You go into town to get something specific and end up coming home without what you wanted, and the kids with a 'Happy Meal'. (Mother from Speke quoted in Andersen *et al.*, 1999)

The Liverpool study focused particularly on the circumstances and attitudes of women in their neighbourhoods. Safety for themselves and their children, the lack of facilities for children and young people and the lack of shops were among their principal concerns. Moreover, the youth clubs which do exist tend to favour boys rather than girls in the activities on offer.

There is an underlying theme of frustration with authority and those from outside which runs through many of the studies. There is the general and familiar complaint that consultation is not the same as involvement and that local people are not really trusted to manage budgets and make important decisions. An implicit polarisation is conveyed in many of the comments in the studies between the well paid 'men in suits', the entrepreneurs of regeneration, and the local activists who are often women. As discussed later, there is often a different view of priorities. Local residents, and perhaps women in particular, may have a greater sense of the 'small things' that could make a difference to people's lives and contrast that sense of what is needed now and is deliverable with more grandiose ideas which seem to get nowhere.

Social cohesion and multiculturalism

In an ethnically mixed neighbourhood, there is a complicated patchwork of overlapping social networks. Here, factors such as length of residence and gender combine with ethnic differences to produce a highly varied pattern of community involvement and activity. The 'community' is multidimensional. In such mixed neighbourhoods, are difference and cohesion compatible? There is a general tendency to focus on racial tensions in poor, ethnically mixed neighbourhoods or to see ethnic heterogeneity as a barrier to collective action and activity. The frustrations of poverty can certainly erupt and be expressed in racial terms and often they do so. Both the London and Nottingham studies allude to such tensions and they clearly remain, particularly in the London neighbourhoods, as a source of division. But the general emphasis is on the positive features of ethnic diversity and the contribution which the dense web of family and neighbourhood links makes to the stock of social capital in the localities. These features are evident from the Nottingham study. Both neighbourhoods have a long history of ethnic diversity and this has produced a gradual tolerance of difference and an evident decline of

Problems with the neighbourhood – the views of women in Speke and Dingle
- Slow repairs and reletting of properties.
- Not enough local shops.
- Too much crime, widespread drug dealing.
- Inadequate facilities for children and young people.
- Lack of discipline among young people.
- Inadequate policing of vandalism, drunkenness or other anti-social behaviour.

Aspects of community

overt racist tensions. One Asian women observed that:

When I used to live down here like when I was 12, 13, we used to get called all sorts, names and stuff and I haven't been called anything for years. If anybody was to say something to me about my race it would hurt me so much, well I'm just not used to it, these things just don't happen. (Asian woman quoted in Silburn et al., 1999)

Nonetheless, ethnic minority groups still face additional layers of disadvantage and discrimination beyond those experienced by the white majority in poor neighbourhoods. This is most keenly felt in the job market but also extends to difficulties of obtaining credit or insurance. These problems are, however, generally associated with the world beyond the local community.

Hyson Green and Forest Fields in Nottingham are the kinds of inner city neighbourhoods traditionally associated with ethnic minority populations. Much of the housing stock is older Victorian terraces. They are busy thoroughfares embedded in the wider urban fabric and adjacent to more affluent, middle-class areas. Here, traffic calming has been an issue in contrast to some of the other neighbourhoods in the mini-programme where increased traffic would be a welcome sign of regeneration. The ethnic mix has also been an important factor in the maintenance of local retailing and other community facilities. Religious and cultural differences have generated a variety of focal points for the different communities – the church, the temple, the mosque:

It's a diverse interesting place, nothing stands still, there's so much happening, you have to be dead to not really feel excited about what's happening.
(Resident of Hyson Green, Nottingham)

While there is a shared sense of spatial boundaries, the social space is experienced in very different ways. There is a strong sense of vibrancy and vitality, a widespread commitment to living there and a degree of optimism about the future. This optimism should not, however, be overstated. While there are more jobs than there were a few years ago and crime rates have fallen, they are still neighbourhoods characterised by high unemployment, high turnover, high population densities, houses in bad condition and lacking amenities, and a generally low quality physical environment.

An important observation made in the Nottingham study concerns the misunderstanding of diversity and difference which references to 'ethnic minorities' can produce. The differences between minorities and majorities can be exaggerated. Alternatively, the misunderstanding can produce a false sense of cohesion and homogeneity within different ethnic groups. There may be significant differences in terms of religion, language and culture, and in terms of income and social class. The African-Caribbean community may be English speaking but originate from a multitude of islands some of which can be hundreds of miles apart. They may have had little contact with one another before settling in England. And, while the Pakistani community is relatively homogeneous in Nottingham, the majority come from a particular part of Kashmir with a tradition and culture distinct from other

Joined-up places?

parts of that country. In a multicultural neighbourhood, therefore, the social glue of kin, neighbour and friendship is considerably more complex than a simple division by broad ethnic groups would indicate. But, again, the study suggests that problems of neighbourhood cohesion which this inevitably creates are at least balanced out by the richness of community activities and organisations generated by the diversity of the area.

Perhaps the most significant feature of ethnic and cultural diversity to emerge from the Nottingham study is the impact on the pattern and reach of social networks. Here, there are contradictory forces at work. On the one hand, ethnic minority organisations and activities are often citywide or national. This deflects energy and commitment from local, area-based groups. On the other hand, these extensive and geographically diffuse networks open up the neighbourhoods to wider influences and allow greater access to formal and informal resources. The density of family ties and strong traditions of mutual aid and assistance produces close-knit communities within the neighbourhoods but they are nevertheless generally outward looking. The pursuance of particular ethnic, religious and cultural interests and activities which are not locally based acts as a bridge into the wider community and is an important conduit for contacts and information. These are features of a multicultural community in an inner city location which are in sharp contrast with some disadvantaged areas in peripheral sites with a predominantly white population. In these latter areas, social networks are often more locally constrained and the community more introverted:

Speke is seen as a place with no through traffic, where people come only if they live or work there, and where the stranger stands out. Isolation and distance from the city centre are deeply felt. (Andersen et al., 1999)

Nevertheless, one consequence of greater involvement in non-locally based activities is an under-representation of ethnic minorities in community-based groups and campaigns. Language barriers and an unfamiliarity with the culture of agendas and formal procedures may be a factor. But there are also important differences of view around issues of race and ethnicity, identity and power which are brought out in the Nottingham study. Referring to discussion within the African-Caribbean population, the Nottingham report comments that:

Some argue that open membership groups cannot reflect the real needs and interests of the African-Caribbean community, will probably be dominated by and run on behalf of white people, and therefore, wittingly or otherwise, oppressive. Involvement in such groups is seen as an unacceptable compromise. Others put the contrary case, that it is only by becoming involved in broader, mainstream groups that the particular needs of the African-Caribbean population can be properly registered.

There is therefore a difficult and delicate balance to be achieved between opposing but related influences in a multicultural community. The same processes which generate rich if sometimes unconnected networks of trust and mutuality which are so important as a foundation for regeneration initiatives also act against fuller representation of ethnic minorities in these locally focused groups and campaigns.

Aspects of community

There is a tension between involvement in wider ethnic minority concerns and commitment to local issues. There are conflicts of time, resources and interest. Greater involvement of minority groups in these mainstream activities is, however, seen as essential to the long-term success of such initiatives.

Particular ethnic groups also represent an important stabilising factor in the neighbourhoods. Through chain migration, a strong commitment to family ties and traditions of mutual support and self-help, minority groups become rooted in particular streets or parts of the neighbourhoods. This acts as an important counterweight to the high turnover which may be a feature of other areas. In this context, the Nottingham researchers emphasise the stabilising influence of the Pakistani community in Hyson Green and Forest Fields:

> *In a district marked by turnover of population, the Pakistani community must be seen as an important stabilising element, a large, linked population who remain in the neighbourhood, because it meets their most important needs and concerns.*

In the same context, a local councillor remarked that the Pakistani community are:

> *... business people, an entrepreneurial class who are making money and spending money within the area. I mean they're everything that inner city communities need in many ways.*

The extensive support mechanisms and webs of family relations built up over time also act to limit the exodus of the more successful and affluent members of the community. Proximity to family, friends and culturally distinct facilities may outweigh the attractions of higher status residential areas. This helps to maintain a middle-class presence (which also includes a small but significant group of white professionals), although this is undoubtedly easier in an inner city neighbourhood where there is a greater variety of dwelling types and amenities than in a peripheral neighbourhood.

Generations and regeneration

Poor areas are often marked by a high degree of age polarisation. The older people who remain are the long-established residents. They may look back on a time when they came as young families. Over time, friends and neighbours have died or moved on. The old community spirit has been eroded with the loss of jobs, shops and familiar faces. Social networks have been weakened as younger newcomers have replaced those who have left. Younger people and younger families appear to lack the discipline of a previous generation. And those who have moved into the area as newcomers, particularly the younger people, may resent the entrenched networks and attitudes of the older locals.

Some element of tension between younger and older people is inevitable in any neighbourhood. Lifestyles and attitudes are bound to collide. These tensions are, however, heightened by poverty, unemployment, high turnover and lack of facilities. While older people may bemoan the exodus of young people who have grown up in the area and see that progressive loss as symptomatic of decline, an influx of families with children from outside may be viewed as equally negative. The age mix in an area has double-edged qualities both

Joined-up places?

contributing to cohesion and revitalisation and creating conflict. Much depends on the degree of population churning and the level of poverty and unemployment. Attitudes vary among adults and older people on the desirability of a mix of ages in the neighbourhood which links to earlier remarks about communities of difference or similarity. For some adults, the cohesive community would be a teenager-free zone. For others, a mix of lifestyles and attitudes, of young and old is an essential ingredient of a healthy neighbourhood:

> *Unless you get the youngsters involved with the older ones you will not mature ... We harp on about the old times, and how good they were, but we should talk to the youngsters ... There is this dreadful resentment of youth, everyone wants them out of their area.*
> (Middle aged resident of Wick, London)

Children, younger and older people may be among those groups who spend most time in their local neighbourhood. Younger people, and particularly those on peripheral or isolated estates, may have limited resources and limited access to opportunities to go further afield. The Liverpool study compares the situation of young people in Dingle, where its inner city location allows access to other neighbourhoods and other facilities, with the feelings of confinement among youth in Speke, which is relatively isolated. A common theme running through all the studies is the lack of facilities for younger people and their frustration at not being listened to. The amenities which are provided are often seen as inappropriate, top-down impositions by adults and those in authority, and primarily designed to get younger people off the street. Young people find themselves at the sharp end of unemployment, deteriorating amenity provision, police attention and stigma. If there is clear evidence on neighbourhood effects, it is in relation to young people. Neighbourhood affects peer group choices, particularly for those in neighbourhoods which are relatively isolated. And young people are more prone to be influenced by their peers than children. Ellen and Turner's review of the US evidence on this issue points to significant neighbourhood effects on adolescents in relation to educational attainment, access to job opportunities via social networks, sexual and criminal behaviour (Ellen and Turner, 1997).

> *The cumulative impact of radical change in relation to employment, training, education, welfare, housing, health, social security, family and criminal justice has meant that the transitionary processes of growing up and passing into 'adulthood' have become more hazardous and insecure.* (Andersen et al., 1999)

Older people, on the other hand, may feel themselves confined and threatened by the behaviour of young people which they are likely to associate with rising crime rates, drug taking and general anti-social behaviour. As local shops disappear and as the streets become less safe, the whole environment becomes more hostile. The general point is that the neighbourhood is experienced in different ways by young and old. They may have different priorities for the regeneration of the area and for themselves. Their social networks will have different qualities. Young people tend to rely on friends and in some cases take refuge in gang culture – a feature of Suttles' defensive community. Older people, on the other hand, may have close and

Aspects of community

long-standing networks of neighbours and friends. The mutual aid and support of youth culture in a poor area will take very different forms and may appear destructive rather than constructive. The mutual aid of elderly people, however, is seen as positively cohesive:

> *Mutual aid characterises the relationships of pensioners on both estates. Shopping for others, 'keeping an eye out' for others, help in illness and support in bereavement were all frequently mentioned.* (Cattell and Evans, 1999)

The London study goes on to describe the activities of a particularly altruistic elderly woman who:

> *... collects all the repeat prescriptions for residents on the estate, takes them to the doctor and the chemist, and delivers them back to the door.* (Cattell and Evans, 1999)

For older people, reciprocity revolves around coping with limited incomes and deteriorating health and capabilities. Young people are preoccupied with a lack of jobs and facilities.

Relationships between the generations vary across the different neighbourhood studies. Generational differences in the Nottingham study are overlaid by culture and religion, and by processes of assimilation. In the London study, the close-knit nature of the older established families and well established networks of pensioners is reflected in thriving social clubs and other facilities. Younger people regard the lack of facilities for them with some resentment and are quite conscious of the link between the absence of suitable venues for their own activities and criminal and anti-social behaviour. The London study makes the important point that young people have no property or tenancy interest in a neighbourhood and, if that is combined with a lack of facilities, there is a very limited basis for any commitment to an area. In what sense can they feel themselves to have a stake in the local neighbourhood? Similarly, the Liverpool team point to the paradox that 'the neighbourhood offers least to those for whom it has the greatest significance'.

> *There's nothing to do here. Yeah, it's dead boring. There's nowhere for us to go so when we get bored we drink. Yeah, we just sit around on the street and then the police come up and they say 'Why don't you go somewhere else?' But there is nowhere for us to go ...* (Young girl from Speke)

Nevertheless, young people are not dismissive of notions of solidarity, community and self-help. What they want most of all is work or the prospect of work when they leave school. They want something to do. They are bored but many feel a strong sense of attachment to their neighbourhoods and value the qualities of reciprocity, mutual support and the importance of having kin and family nearby. They are also acutely aware of the way their own behaviour may be perceived as threatening by older people and of the dangers of hard drugs on those younger than themselves.

Younger and older people, at either ends of the life course, experience decline and disadvantage in different ways. On the verge of adulthood, young people face the frustrations of joblessness and the difficulties of gaining adequate and affordable housing. They feel powerless and lacking voice in circumstances where many are fully aware that their behaviour is seen as symptomatic of the decline of cohesion and community. Older people reflect on better times, of community lost and can often remember periods when jobs were relatively plentiful and the area did not suffer from the stigma which it now has. Youth are regarded as often lacking social discipline and social control, and as a threat to the safety and security of their elders. Nonetheless, older people acknowledge the corrosive effects of the loss of young people for the future of the community. And young and old share many of the same views as to what is required for the regeneration of the area. For young people, it is primarily jobs but the lack of other facilities and their sense of exclusion from community life adds to a more general sense of despair and powerlessness. The social networks of mutuality and self-help among older people are important if declining elements of the social glue in a community. They add stability in vulnerable and precarious circumstances. But, as the Liverpool study observes, while 'the elders themselves remain embedded it is the "top soil" of local communities [which] is being eroded'.

Aspects of community: conclusion

What do these studies tell us about the nature of the social relationships in these neighbourhoods? To what extent can these poor neighbourhoods be regarded as socially disorganised, as lacking cohesion? First, they illustrate, as have previous studies, that in poor neighbourhoods there is ample evidence of strong bonds of reciprocity, of powerful feelings of attachment and commitment, and of continuing resilience and optimism in the face of adversity, decline and disillusionment. Second, the research also shows that social cohesion can take different forms. Policymakers tend to think of the close-knit community of mutual aid and friendly neighbours when referring to social cohesion. Cohesion is inherently positive. But, within our neighbourhoods, there is also the cohesion which can be inward-looking and suspicious of outsiders. And there is the cohesion of youth culture which can be perceived and experienced as anti-social by others.

These are not areas which lack the elements of social cohesion. There are significant differences within and between these neighbourhoods in relation to stability and turnover, and in the nature and strength of the ties which bind people together. There are differences of view regarding the positive attributes of diversity in building community cohesion and commitment as opposed to the solidarity of similarity in relation to such factors as age, ethnicity and stage in the life course. But there appear to be a shared sense of belonging and a shared sense of what a 'good' neighbourhood needs which cut across age, gender and ethnic group. To the extent that dense webs of relationships, trust and familiarity constitute an important dimension of social capital these areas have rich resources to draw on. When residents are asked about 'community', they refer to the positive qualities of the people. What are lacking are the other elements which can be mobilised to positive effect, namely, real material resources in terms of jobs and income.

Women emerge as key actors in formal and informal activities. Action often mobilises around issues of child care and schooling. Children are a pivotal element in social networks. Older women maintain older,

Aspects of community

established networks of mutual aid and assistance. But voluntary activity requires time and energy which many women find difficult to sustain because of lack of child care and crèche facilities and the daily grind of having to cope with very limited financial resources.

Heterogeneity, particularly in relation to ethnicity, is often used as an indicator of disorganisation and disunity. But the Nottingham study emphasises ethnic diversity as a positive element of community vitality. In these areas at least, ethnic diversity produces a complex web of relationships, activities and focal points within a neighbourhood. The prioritisation of cultural or religous links and activities which are citywide or national can, however, weaken commitment to local groups and area-based interests. Nevertheless, the community tends to be more outward-looking because of the wider networks of ethnic minorities – social ties reach outside and are important bridges to the world beyond the neighbourhood. In this context, there are also important differences between an inner city neighbourhood embedded in the wider urban fabric and those in peripheral locations. The Nottingham research shows that some ethnic minorities can be an important stabilising influence in areas of generally high turnover through their greater social investment in the neighbourhood.

3 The neighbourhood environment

Neighbourhood functions

In its early twentieth-century conception, the neighbourhood was cellular, bounded, inwardly focused and relatively self-contained. It emphasised the environment as a major determinant of residential quality of life. The concept of neighbourhood, which was adopted in much American urban planning and in new town planning in Britain and elsewhere, derived from the fact that there were concerns in the first decades of the century about the effects of urbanisation, and the neighbourhood concept was an attempt to counter these by promoting neighbourliness, identity with primary groups and places, order and dignity. The neighbourhood was intended to create a physical place that was coterminous with a sense of community through providing a setting in which there were opportunities for leisure, recreation and social interaction, and an environment that was safe, secure and protected. It was proposed by Clarence Perry in 1929 (referred to in Brower 1996) that a neighbourhood should comprise six elements:

- school: an elementary school with appropriate population size
- boundaries: bounded by arterial roads
- open spaces: small parks and playgrounds
- central site: for community institutions
- local shops: one or more shopping areas on the periphery
- internal street system: to facilitate internal circulation.

The neighbourhood approach to planning has been criticised on a number of grounds, with the main thrust of these arguments against the neighbourhood being twofold. First, the family basis and cultural homogeneity assumed in the concept of the neighbourhood no longer exist, and each social and ethnic group has differing lifestyles and values and its own residential needs. Second, the city-dweller derives satisfaction from the whole (non-place) urban realm so that social networks are not congruent with the neighbourhood and limited satisfaction is derived from the neighbourhood's physical forms.

A different way of considering the neighbourhood environment is offered by Brower (1996), who also helps us to understand why neighbourhoods might still matter to residents, despite the availability of the wider urban arena. For Brower, housing units and related facilities serve to meet residential functions, which are activities and meanings associated with housing:

- shelter: affordable and effective protection
- housekeeping: completing tasks such as food preparation, cleaning clothes, waste disposal, etc. with reasonable cost and effort
- accommodation: providing sufficient space and facilities for domestic activities such as play space
- connection: connection to employment and services and opportunities for co-operative connections with other households
- recreation: the opportunity to relax and re-create oneself

The neighbourhood environment

- meaning: the values of the householder must be reflected in the character, appearance and conditions of use of the housing, thus fostering belonging, attachment and advocacy.

Others have suggested more strictly psycho-social functions such as identity, privacy, escape, interaction, affiliation, belonging and social recognition. Neighbourhoods in this formulation are both social and spatial; they consist of neighbours' attitudes and behaviours on the one hand, and the physical attributes and places (facilities) which satisfy these attitudes and behaviours on the other.

Brower goes on to construct a model in which the neighbourhood has three dimensions pertaining to the physical environment, social interaction and the extent of diversity of lifestyles present in the neighbourhood. He called these three elements 'ambience', 'engagement' and 'choicefulness':

- ambience: the nature, mix and intensity of land uses and the appearance and form of the physical environment

- engagement: the nature and extent of interaction among residents and the presence of facilities and features of the neighbourhood which encourage this

- choicefulness: alternative locations, lifestyles and living arrangements in the neighbourhood.

In each of these domains, there are no arrangements that will suit everyone. But past studies allow one to identify some key elements for all, or for different kinds of, neighbourhoods.

Quality and type of environment (ambience)

What sort of flavour or tone do people seek from their residential environment? Studies have found people to vary as to whether they are looking for tranquillity in the residential environment or activity: the former being associated with a preference for low density, homogeneous areas with greenery; the latter existing alongside a preference for an environment of historic and/or stylish buildings. In both cases, people agree on a need for good quality, adequate and convenient public transport, and essential maintenance to keep the neighbourhood looking clean and tidy. But there are questions being asked about whether people these days prefer their neighbourhoods to be purely residential or to contain other non-residential functions and services, either to remove the home–work divide, or to reduce car dependency, or to enhance opportunities for social interaction.

Social interaction (engagement)

People's satisfaction with their neighbourhood is often found to be closely related to whether they consider it to be a friendly place, and to how they rate various attributes of their neighbours. But, although people want friendly neighbours, they do not necessarily want intimate neighbours, though in some neighbourhoods closer relations with neighbours will be the norm. Thus, in many neighbourhoods, people will want to know one another and have neighbours who are outgoing and friendly; but they also want privacy and do not want to feel any pressure to socialise; in some neighbourhoods, people want to go beyond this to a more intimate form of engagement in which residents are involved in

Joined-up places?

community affairs and where people take care of one another; in other neighbourhoods, residents are looking for opportunities to engage with new, diverse people and have an active social life near home.

Social interaction is underpinned by three attributes of the neighbourhood environment. First, by a safe environment in which to engage. Engagement won't happen if the environment is poorly kept and conveys feelings of being unsafe. Second, familiarity and engagement are associated with residential stability, as is neighbourhood satisfaction. Third, one needs places and activities that bring people together in the neighbourhood. But, whilst shared places and activities are important, within different neighbourhoods, residents' views will vary to differing degrees as to which amenities are important and where they should be located. Residents may want amenities to meet household needs, children's needs or individual and cultural needs.

Choice and diversity (choicefulness)

A consideration of the dimension of 'choicefulness' can be broken down into three elements. People want to feel that they live in their neighbourhoods by choice, not by constraint. For most people, having some choice in the matter of relocation into the neighbourhood is important. People also want to feel that their neighbourhood would be chosen by others; that it has a reputation as a desirable place to live and is a place where people they respect or would want to emulate would live, and where property values appreciate. Lastly, there is a dichotomy between people who prefer the homogeneity of suburbia, and those who resist the conformity of suburbia or who simply prefer the diversity of inner city, urban living. People can also be divided as to whether they prefer neighbours who are 'down to earth' or neighbours who are 'sophisticated', with both sorts being possible in suburban situations.

Having reviewed the components and qualities of neighbourhoods and their environments, we now consider those aspects of neighbourhood environments which featured in the eight study areas.

Community facilities

All the areas studied had some amenities and community facilities either within or immediately adjacent to the neighbourhood. There was, however, a lot of variation in the extent and quality of these, with some of these circumstances having important effects on the neighbourhood.

Shops

The two Teesside estates illustrate the problems facing small neighbourhoods in being unable to sustain retail facilities. One estate of around 800 houses which was two miles from the town centre had no shops, and the other estate of around 600 houses had only a post office and a general store, though it was only a quarter-of-a-mile from the town centre. The latter fact may compensate for the lack of a local shop, but it does not overcome the loss of shop, or shops, as a focal point for the community.

Both of the estates in London and the two neighbourhoods in Liverpool had suffered the loss of shops through closure. The Trowbridge estate in Hackney now had only one small shop; it had become a 'quiet suburb', appreciated by

The neighbourhood environment

some residents but not by others who remember the area as a lively place full of shops. The Keir Hardie estate in Newham had witnessed a sharp decline in its shops in the last decade, so that very few shops remain. The two neighbourhoods studied in Liverpool had both seen supermarkets shut, in one case a Co-op and in the other a Kwik Save. The Speke area with nearly 6,000 dwellings now has no supermarket and is eight miles from the city centre. Both Liverpool neighbourhoods had central shopping areas, but these now had very few shops and those shops which remained had seen their trade decline. Speke had lost shoe shops, utility shops and Woolworths.

The closures with the most significant impacts were those of supermarkets and banks. Three of the neighbourhoods studied had lost banking facilities in the last few years. This compounded the loss of major shops, so that together these events meant that neighbourhoods became less self-sufficient. Life became harder and more costly for residents having to travel elsewhere with children on public transport to buy many essential items. Furthermore, there was a tangible feeling in Speke that people travelled to other neighbourhoods for the use of a bank, and then did their shopping there, thus further disadvantaging the local economy. The credit union, while seen as helpful, did not compensate for the loss of services and spillover retail benefits of having a local bank.

The two Nottingham neighbourhoods, on the other hand, have a better range of local shops, though they have declined in number and are vulnerable because of changed patterns of shopping at large supermarkets. But the positive signs are there and are not just due to the fact that these are inner city neighbourhoods, but, as noted earlier in this report, are also a result of the ethnic mix which has helped maintain local retail facilities. The fact that the local neighbourhood contains communities with particular tastes and needs has meant that 'niche-marketing' has grown with specialist travel agents, clothes shops, butchers and bakers. Local social diversity and non-mainstream tastes, therefore, have enabled a local retail sector to develop. There may be things other neighbourhoods could learn from this experience.

The Nottingham studies are also instructive for the account they present of the importance of the retail sector as activists and leaders within the local community. As we shall see, the local shopkeepers recognised themselves as key stakeholders in the local neighbourhood, with a mutual interest with the residents in seeing the environment improved.

Schools

Most of the neighbourhoods had several primary schools and one or two secondary schools. Low standards and a poor state of repair were issues, though, for many of them. This was found to be important not only for the children directly but also because the quality of education, even for people with few resources, affected their attachment to the area. In Nottingham, the inner city schools in the study neighbourhoods were poor performers in terms of qualifications outcomes, but the schools suffered from a lack of resources and teaching difficulties caused by disruptions consequent on a high residential turnover and unsettled children in the neighbourhood. Some parents had the resources to respond to this situation by

Joined-up places?

sending their children to suburban schools. Others, namely Pakistani parents, ran extra classes in basic subjects, thus turning a disadvantage to an advantage and enhancing the neighbourhood's social and human capital. In the case of only one of the schools in the eight study areas was there a significant forward strategy for the enhancement of the local education service.

In the absence of other facilities, schools provided a meeting place for parents. In the two Teesside study areas, however, there were no schools, and, in the case of St Hilda's in Middlesbrough, the closure (and subsequent demolition) of the local primary school had led to despondency on the part of the local residents: they now believed the local authority was going to close the estate down altogether; and they watched the slow vandalisation of the empty school as a reminder of their destiny.

Halls and clubs

In general, the neighbourhoods seemed to be adequately served with health services (doctors, dentists, chemists, etc.), advice centres, job and training centres and community halls. Things which were less often sufficiently provided were recreation and leisure facilities, social clubs, amenities for young people, child care services, and local public and statutory service outlets. Many adults in these neighbourhoods wanted social clubs for relaxation, not necessarily pubs, though, if they had pubs in the area, there was a lively pub life. Residents in London remembered a period in the past when youth and social clubs were more common than today. Such clubs brought the community together, as one interviewee in London said: 'Until we have a place where everybody can meet, we don't have a community'. Thus, the provision of community centres or halls was not seen as sufficient to meet the neighbourhood's social needs, though, as a foundation, there was an association made (for example, clearly by the residents of Norton Grange, Stockton) between the provision of community facilities and the presence of 'community'. However, in the case of one of the London estates, a situation had developed whereby a community hall had been provided for local pensioners after a successful campaign by them but they now would not permit other, younger residents to use it. A successful resolution of this conflict, which reflected deeper divisions in the community, had yet to be found.

As noted in the section on women in the community, mothers wanted more for their children to do. They also wanted more child care facilities. In some neighbourhoods, child care was available only on a weekly basis to allow women to attend training courses, but with nothing to enable them to take a job. All adults wanted more for youth to do, recognising the need for different things for different age groups, such as art classes, sports clubs and drop-in centres. Youth themselves wanted clubs under their control, not clubs premised on an interpretation of them as 'problems'. Youth wanted their own place and clubs which met their needs, otherwise they had no stake in the area. Similar comments were made about how social housing allocations policies also failed to give young people a stake in the future of the area (see below).

Public services

The presence of public services in disadvantaged areas is extremely important for a number of reasons. Often, public services used to be a noticeable local feature, and the gradual closure and withdrawal of public agencies contribute significantly to the general impression and reality of closure and loss. Many disadvantaged areas have felt the effects of public service rationalisation on local authority services but also on other public services such as water and fire protection. Overall, there is less local public presence than there used to be and this reinforces the view that the functions of these neighbourhoods are narrowing in scope. It also makes a lot of day-to-day tasks more difficult where the non-local presence of public services is combined (as it often is) with poor transport services to other parts of the city where such services are now based.

Residents noticed whether the local authority and other public services had offices or bases in the neighbourhood: this was understood to affect the quality of service and to send messages about the authorities' confidence in the area. However, in the absence of services, self-help had proved an important means of acquiring services and of defining the nature of the community. Self-provision, for example, of a credit union in Dingle and of a well-woman clinic and a credit union in Speke, had convinced residents that the community had the necessary fight and spirit to create a future for itself, but these self-help measures had also cemented anti-establishment views by reinforcing the residents' views that they would get things only if they fought for them or did them themselves.

The knock-on effects of public service withdrawal and the need for better public services locally are illustrated in the Speke area of Liverpool, where residents were convinced that crime was a significant factor in the closure of shops and the post office. They wanted a better community police service to tackle this problem, as well as other improvements to the neighbourhood such as quicker letting of empty houses, better street lighting and more organised facilities for children. Two major local problems, closure of amenities and crime, were connected to the quality of the local environment and the (non)localised nature of public services.

In general, many needy residents in these deprived areas found public bureaucracies too inflexible in their rules and arrangements to be of much assistance to them. If a local presence and a decentralised structure for the delivery of public services could be combined with local flexibility in policies and budgets, then poor communities might feel the public sector was on their side:

If you go to the Social Services, to the people who are supposed to count, the response is that they haven't got the money, can't get the money, the grants have run out, you'll have to wait until next year until they get some money – so you just don't go there. (Resident, Liverpool)

Social interaction in the neighbourhood

Facilities within the neighbourhood were found to be important for a number of reasons: they strengthened residents' attachment to the area; they directly affected continuity of residence, e.g. in the case of schools; they supported the formation of social networks; and they enhanced residents' familiarity with one another. Casual meeting places, such as schools, markets, shops and clubs, were found to be

Joined-up places?

important in bringing residents together, even if only briefly. Having an amenity such as a nearby canal (as in the case of one of the London estates) which many people used in the summer increased familiarity and brought the community together.

Community facilities and festivals were identified as means of enhancing social interaction, particularly in order to get people to mix beyond their most immediate neighbours. As interviewees in London said: 'We need something to bring all groups together' and 'Our sense of community could be improved ... but we don't have the facilities to bring it about'.

Social interaction among co-residents was also influenced by housing design and layout, pedestrianisation and residential turnover. In the two estates in London, the comparative experience of previous tower block residents was instructive. Smaller developments (e.g. the Wick Village, Trowbridge) of terraced houses and squares, with pedestrian routes through the estate to school past people's front doors and windows, helped transform social relations in the neighbourhood. The new design and layout provided opportunities for casual communication among residents and facilitated the improved control and socialisation of children. Similarly, Kier Hardie residents living in small squares appreciated opportunities for sitting out and socialising with neighbours in the summer. Similar effects of small-scale landscaping features which provided sitting out areas in the summer were reported on the St Hilda's estate in Middlesbrough.

The inner city neighbourhoods in Nottingham had advantages and disadvantages with regard to social interaction. The street layout with culs-de-sac and the fact that people walk rather than use their cars mean that people say 'hello' to one another and look out for one another. Further, a plethora of focal points allowed people to form different, overlapping social networks. But, in streets where residential turnover was higher, people didn't get to know one another sufficiently for trust to develop between them and acquaintance to develop into friendship before they moved on; in these circumstances, longer-term residents tended to withdraw.

A sense of place and feelings of loss

Residents in several of the study areas witnessed the decline of their neighbourhoods and some felt a keen sense of loss as a result. This particularly applied to the neighbourhoods in Liverpool and the one in Middlesbrough:

> *We've lost the school now ... We've got a terrific amount of brilliant listed buildings over here but they're going to rack and ruin. I mean the Custom House, the cathedral – it's terrible what we're losing. This was old Middlesbrough but we've got nothing and nobody's interested ... It's a shame, we're losing our heritage, we are going to have nothing to give our kids any more.*
> (Resident, St Hilda's, Middlesbrough)

In Dingle in Liverpool, small-scale new housing developments were acknowledged, but could not compensate for the sense that the main neighbourhood facilities were declining, with major retailers closing. In the Speke area, random dereliction and piecemeal improvements over the years had disrupted the original plan of an ordered, homogenous, newly developed neighbourhood. There was a sense of

The neighbourhood environment

loss and betrayal for the closure of shops and nearby factories.

Empty and derelict properties had a strong impact on residents' perceptions of their neighbourhoods. They sometimes could not understand why there were so many unused properties when they knew young people wanted homes and, in an area like Speke, residents felt that other people's view of their neighbourhood was of an area full of voids. Residents in St Hilda's, Middlesbrough were also concerned about the number of 'empties' (residential and non-residential) and their effect upon their own and other people's view of the estate. Even on the Norton Grange estate in Stockton-on-Tees, recently refurbished, one of the main feelings about the neighbourhood was the reappearance of empty houses.

In these circumstances, residents identified a failure on the part of the major stakeholders to manage their neighbourhoods. This is summed up in the view of one Speke resident that 'they've just left it to fall to bits'. In their case, this comment was primarily aimed at housing managers for allowing the occurrence of empty properties and for taking far too long to do housing repairs, which added to the sense of dereliction. But the charge was also laid against the retail sector and the council in general. A failure to look after public parks and many green areas such as large grass verges had allowed dumping to take place, valued facilities such as tennis courts had been removed, and large areas had become 'no go areas' for many people. The Trowbridge estate in Hackney also had 'dusty open spaces' awaiting further regeneration. At the heart of their neighbourhoods were unwelcoming places and, in the eyes of Liverpool residents, special projects and public consultation exercises did not compensate for the lack of good quality public services.

Neighbourhoods such as St Hilda's in Middlesbrough demonstrate the importance of older, historic buildings to the residents' sense of place. For some, the neighbourhood had declined since the demolition of St Hilda's itself, the old church which served the area. The old town hall at the centre of the neighbourhood is now almost derelict, as are other public buildings such as the Catholic cathedral, but the point applies also to Victorian pubs and old factory buildings. This deterioration of older and in some cases 'landmark' buildings led residents to feel a loss of their heritage; a loss of pride, status and identity in the area; a sense of lack of control over their neighbourhood; and a lack of confidence in the council's commitment to the area. In London, residents of the Keir Hardie estate had fought to save St Luke's Church which is now a community centre with business spaces, doctors' surgeries and public spaces. They defended this building because of their sense of collective history (it was known as the 'Cathedral of the East End', and had survived the Blitz) and because they had personal associations with it through marriages, christenings and burials. Their view was:

St Luke's is a landmark. When they pull things down, you think another part of your life has gone. (Resident, Keir Hardie estate, London)

The loss of a neighbourhood's past through the destruction of its buildings had a crucial impact on residents' views as to whether the neighbourhood had a future.

Joined-up places?

Big visions and modest projects: community-led environmental improvements

The two inner city Nottingham neighbourhoods demonstrate how environmental improvements instigated by residents and local traders can bring a range of benefits both directly through the enhancement of the environment, but also because the process of physical improvement can lead to social development. The local projects described in the study were as follows. First, the installation of security gates across the back alleys in the Forest Fields area in order to reduce crime. This was led by a group of volunteer residents who formed a project committee, which involved seeking the approval of all residents as well as local resident management of the gates once installed. Second, the formation of the Birkin Patch Improvement Association in a definable set of streets containing 420 houses. The group started by cleaning up back alleys and the Association is involved in installing security gates on those alleys, obtaining traffic calming measures in the area and funding a community centre. The process has involved consultation with the residents of all 420 houses.

The Hyson Green Traders' Association has sought to revitalise the Hyson Green neighbourhood, enhance trade and support local traders in a number of ways. The status of the area in the eyes of residents and other people is seen as a key to successful trade. The Association has undertaken a number of activities including fighting to keep the local swimming baths open; putting a historic plaque on the Hyson Green Market and trying to give people a sense of history and place; helping to run the Hyson Green Festival, which again has improved people's sense of place and got the area good publicity; and providing a business planning service to local shop owners. The Traders' Association has also organised the Hyson Green in Bloom project which has expanded from the placement of hanging baskets on shops, offices and public buildings to the hanging of baskets on their homes by residents. This award-winning project is funded by residents, traders, local businesses and the local authority and has again brought publicity for the neighbourhood and helped maintain trade.

The benefits of these local environmental projects have been as follows.

- Good publicity for the neighbourhoods.

- The process of implementation enhances communication among residents.

- Outside the projects themselves, people get to know one another and have something to talk about.

- Intergenerational assistance has been forthcoming between neighbours to enable everyone to play a part in the projects where resident responsibilities are involved.

- People feel happier about their neighbourhood, walk about in it more and use the local shops.

- Modest but visible improvements for which the residents themselves are largely responsible have led to further action on other issues. The boost in morale has fed into other beneficial activities.

The neighbourhood environment

- People feel more secure in their local neighbourhood and this has fostered social cohesion.

- Community confidence and expectations are raised so that local people aim higher and won't be satisfied with small returns on their efforts.

The elements which have contributed to the projects' success have included the following.

- The community has owned the projects rather than having solutions imposed on it.

- Continual efforts at communicating with the less active residents.

- Clearly defined areas with dense street patterns within which to implement the projects.

- Dedicated and determined leadership which has focused on achievable ends.

- A good response from the local council to the residents' self-help and hands-on approach to environmental problems. The council hasn't felt undermined, threatened or hostile to the projects.

- Decentralised area management within the local council has meant that flexibility has been possible in the use of local budgets in order to allocate funds to the projects.

Neighbourhood image and exclusion

Boundedness and isolation

Neighbourhoods can be well defined by the style and similarity of their buildings and by the clarity of their borders. Physical homogeneity and boundary definition can contribute to a sense of place and community, as they do for the elder residents of Speke, but the problem facing many of the neighbourhoods studied is that boundedness had become isolation:

> *The main problem is we're an island on our own. We've got to leave the area for anything we want.* (Resident, Keir Hardie estate, London)

> *We have got a very narrow perception of distance because we are an island ... It takes a good 45 minutes from town, that distance in our minds because of where we come from is a huge distance.* (Resident, Speke, Liverpool)

The sense of isolation could be acute, as in the case of an outer estate like Speke, eight miles from the city centre with few roads in or out of the neighbourhood and poor transport links with the rest of the city. The two London estates are also physically isolated, but, in the case of the Trowbridge estate, this was seen as an advantage given the reputation of its host borough, Hackney. For the Keir Hardie estate in Newham, on the other hand, isolation was a disadvantage as it reinforced the fact that the estate had not benefited from the regeneration of London's docklands.

For the Keir Hardie estate in London and the Speke estate in Liverpool, the absence of leisure facilities and the poor road and transport links contributed to a situation where outsiders rarely visited the estates, making them, in the eyes of residents and other people, 'out on a limb' or 'on the edge'. The use of such terms, and others such as the label 'over the border' as used for the St Hilda's neighbourhood in Middlesbrough, conflates a statement about the physical

Joined-up places?

situation of the neighbourhoods with a comment on the reputation of the areas. St Hilda's demonstrates that a neighbourhood which is close to a town centre can still be isolated if it is bounded by non-residential land uses on all sides.

The contrast is provided by the neighbourhoods studied in Nottingham, where closeness to the city centre is allied with good bus services and a main road through the middle of the neighbourhood. The opportunity for outside visits is therefore present, added to which the local traders and residents have endeavoured to give outsiders reasons to visit through improvements in the environment and shopping amenities. Some areas, though deprived, have a better chance of successful reversal than others. Physically isolated areas need greater efforts on the part of authorities and agencies to provide good links with the wider urban area and to give other city dwellers reasons to go there. Dingle in Liverpool, which already has several bus routes, is about to get a light rail link; Speke is not.

Image

All the neighbourhoods under study suffered from a negative image. These reputations had historic roots, were the result of particular unsavoury events, or were part of the perceptions of wider areas to which the neighbourhoods were linked.

Negative images of areas last for decades if not centuries, sometimes well beyond the period and reasons from which they were originally derived. Both the St Hilda's neighbourhood in Middlesbrough and the Keir Hardie estate in London had reputations linked to their older function as dockland areas, whilst the Trowbridge estate had a historic negative image because of the presence of anti-social industries such as chemical and dye works. The Norton Grange estate in Stockton-on-Tees had a reputation derived from its origins as a slum clearance estate in the 1930s, rehousing the poorest, disadvantaged families from the inner urban area. In these cases, images from past reports which detailed the poverty and social problems of the areas and described them as being in 'extreme social need' still persisted.

The Hyson Green area of Nottingham acquired its reputation for violence and crime much more recently during the 1980s when civil disturbances occurred in and around the Hyson Green flats complex; the flats had now gone, but the reputation remained.

Some neighbourhoods derive their images from the reputations of wider areas, so perhaps one should not expect action within the neighbourhoods to change things. In the case of both Liverpool and London, television dramas had also made a contribution. The two estates in London were seen as typical of the East End (as portrayed on *EastEnders*), and assumed to be white, working class, macho, racist and closed, though this was also partly because of them historically being 'occupational communities' and, in the case of the Trowbridge estate, being seen as part of the 'estate culture' of Hackney.

Dingle in Liverpool (another neighbourhood with a docks connection in the past) suffers from the image of a working-class area of 'have-nots' portrayed in the television series *Bread*, and from sharing its L8 postcode with Toxteth where the riots of the early 1980s occurred. For many of the residents it is not part of Toxteth, but, to outsiders, it can be seen as the same area of violence and danger; as in the case of Hyson

The neighbourhood environment

Green, images of civil disturbance linger and are perpetuated by the media. Just as the London estates are thought of in terms of the conventional caricature of the East End, so young Liverpudlians, because they come from poor areas, are tainted with the wider image of working-class people from Liverpool. Young people felt they were living in a 'marked community', summed up in the following comments from young residents: 'To them you're just a Scouser ... on TV though the scousers are always really bad people' and 'People say "get back where you're from"'.

In several neighbourhoods, residents saw negative images being perpetuated by the media and by the local council. Newspapers got good copy from all the unsavoury happenings in deprived areas; they had their favourite topics (robberies and violent crimes) and their favourite locations to report them from. Local authorities were also seen to perpetuate bad images, though often for the 'good' reason of accessing funds for regeneration and other programmes.

Residents felt they had to defend their neighbourhoods, but, in some cases, they had been able to go further and promote a more positive image of their neighbourhood. This had been attempted through the production of community newspapers (e.g. in Dingle), a change of estate name (e.g. Norton Grange) and through the activism of local residents and traders, including the mounting of neighbourhood festivals (e.g. Hyson Green).

Two major factors which had to be overcome, however, were the dominant effects of a poor physical image, and the need to get outsiders to visit these neighbourhoods. In the case of the Trowbridge estate in Hackney, physical regeneration was considered to have been successful in changing the image of the neighbourhood, but only in the eyes of those who had cause to go there, which was not many people. Similarly, residents on Norton Grange in Stockton reported that most people in the town believed nothing changes, but those who had come back to visit the estate were pleasantly surprised. Young people in the Liverpool neighbourhoods were clear that the negative external image of the area was largely perpetuated by a poor physical environment:

People who come down here don't see it as a nice place ... they only see the shit we live in.
(Resident, Speke, Liverpool)

Liverpool residents wanted comprehensive improvement in the housing and environment in order to change their neighbourhoods' image. In talking about empty houses in disrepair, they said:

If they did all the houses. Yeah, make it look pretty ... people aren't afraid of pretty things.
(Resident, Liverpool)

Overcoming others' fear of the areas is part of the answer, but young people from Speke also wanted to give outsiders a reason to visit through the provision of facilities for all in order to overcome negative myths; they wanted to open the place up and make it a place worth visiting, linking physical improvements with integration into the wider city.

Area discrimination

The fact that neighbourhoods have poor images and bad reputations has serious consequences for residents. The studies provided indications and illustrations of many of these effects.

Joined-up places?

The social effects of a poor image were felt by schoolchildren. In Dingle, teenage girls reported that the mothers of friends at school wouldn't let their daughters come to the area to visit them. Adults in the study areas had less concrete proof, but also felt that friends were less likely to visit the neighbourhoods, or consider moving to them because of the bad image.

Economically, the difficulties which existed surrounded 'address discrimination' in the labour market. Residents of some of the neighbourhoods, such as those in inner Nottingham, felt that their address precluded them from getting interviews or job offers. Some residents, for example in St Hilda's, had derived circumstantial evidence of this discrimination by testing how well they did in the application and selection process for jobs when they altered their addresses. On top of this, residents of these neighbourhoods faced higher insurance costs and difficulties in obtaining credit. Some people had been denied credit and insurance.

The provision of services to the neighbourhoods also deteriorated, or was worse because of their poor image. Examples were reported in the studies of being denied goods for hire; paying more for telephone connections; not being allowed to register at some doctors' surgeries; taxis not taking fares into these areas; and not being permitted to have a pet from a rescue home. Public services were also seen as culprits. Schools were accused of having low expectations of children from these neighbourhoods and not really trying with them, and the children faced stigmatising attitudes from teachers and fellow pupils if they attended school elsewhere (a necessity in some cases). In St Hilda's, Middlesbrough, there were even reports of petitions from other schools to prevent St Hilda's children attending after the local school in the area closed down.

The police were in some cases considered to be offering these neighbourhoods a poorer service, with slow response times to calls and unhelpful attitudes on arrival at crime scenes. More significantly, there was a suspicion that the police and local authorities were complicit in a strategy to corral and confine drug dealers and prostitutes into these neighbourhoods, both because these are places where such behaviours are deserved or considered normal and in order to keep such problems away from other parts of the urban area. Knowing where the main problems were also made policing easier.

The neighbourhood environment: conclusion

The studies have shown that the neighbourhood environment still matters a great deal to these disadvantaged communities. The elements of the neighbourhood conceived in early planning concepts are still in one way or another desired, though not always present. Similarly, residents would prefer their neighbourhoods to satisfy a range of residential functions, but changing social patterns of shopping, leisure and recreation, together with the significant costs involved in providing facilities, meant that these neighbourhoods were no longer self-sufficient for many of the functions people sought from them.

In several ways, the neighbourhood as a physical entity has social consequences. The neighbourhood was shown to matter in the strong feelings of loss felt by residents as elements of their neighbourhoods declined or

The neighbourhood environment

disappeared. The closure of public and commercial facilities and the decline in the environment gave the overwhelming impression to residents that these neighbourhoods were on a downward trajectory. The impacts were greater where historic landmark buildings, which in some way signified the neighbourhood identity, were allowed to deteriorate. The fact that such significant decline of important local buildings and facilities was allowed to happen raises questions about how these neighbourhoods have been treated, and the lack of power on the part of residents, despite a succession of local regeneration initiatives over the years. Rather than being cohesive, the experience of loss led many residents to the view that things were 'falling to bits' locally.

The design and maintenance of neighbourhoods are extremely important. Housing design and estate layout influenced the socialisation of children and the degree of informal interaction among residents. Furthermore, people withdrew from public spaces that were not maintained, and the failure to maintain the housing stock quickly produced a sense of decline and offered opportunities for vandalism. Residents wanted public services based in their neighbourhoods; they were convinced that this improved the services, but more than this it gave a clear signal of local authority commitment to the area. The social effects of environmental improvements were greatest where residents and local traders were involved in their organisation and provision, but this was again assisted by local decentralised service provision as close contact with the authorities and local flexible service budgets were key elements of successful local environmental projects. A partnership with the local community for local public services seemed to be what was desired.

Poor neighbourhoods suffered poor images for a number of reasons, and these images and reputations had concrete effects on the fortunes of residents both socially and economically and in terms of the provision of public and private services to the neighbourhood. Concerted efforts were required with the media and with the local authority to try to change the image of poor neighbourhoods. However, in some cases, these images were tied up with the image of the wider urban area, so that local strategies alone would not suffice. Two key elements necessary for image enhancement were physical improvements and interaction with people from other parts of the town or city. The two were needed together if the 'socio-spatial invisibility' of many of these poor neighbourhoods (Bartley, 1998) was to be reversed. Physical and social isolation had to be overcome if prejudices were to be dispelled. This was important in both directions. Adequate transport infrastructure and services were lacking to such an extent that neighbourhood residents felt cut-off or at an enormous distance from other parts of the urban area. In the other direction, residents were aware that people from elsewhere rarely visited their neighbourhoods, had not seen what changes had taken place, and, what is more, had no reason to visit. Most of the study neighbourhoods had not been integrated into the urban fabric.

4 The experience of regeneration

Undergoing regeneration

All of the areas studied have undergone programmes of redevelopment and regeneration over the past two decades, and are currently the subject of a range of regeneration initiatives, as shown in Table 1.

Community involvement and community priorities

People held differing views about the issue of community involvement in regeneration programmes, though most supported the approach. For some, community involvement was so fundamental that it went without saying that it should be part and parcel of regeneration. As well as seeing such involvement as a right, some people also saw it as a moral duty, but other people took a contrasting perspective and considered that resident involvement should occur only if it could be demonstrated to have a real input to decisions and to have the scope to make a difference. Involvement should not take place so that the professionals could say they had consulted the community, nor because it was assumed that consultation would make the community happier about the process:

There are a number of occasions when local people have said, 'This programme is crap'. But I have had to give it the point, because it has gone through the motions, it has done what it was asked to do in terms of 'Did it consult?' Yes, we still thought it was rubbish but it did come and consult, so it got its consultation points.
(Resident, Liverpool)

One of the justifications given for community involvement in regeneration was

Table 1 Summary of regeneration initiatives in the areas studied

Area	Regeneration initiatives
Trowbridge, Hackney	Part of Hackney Council's 1990s' Comprehensive Estates Initiative (CEI). Includes housing redevelopment, provision of community facilities and employment and training schemes. The wider area is subject to economic regeneration, including the redevelopment of a dog track stadium and a new international passenger terminal at Hackney Wick.
Keir Hardie, Newham	Part of the Canning Town Partnership Single Regeneration Area (SRB). Objectives include housing refurbishment and redevelopment, economic development and community development. The adjacent area has received Challenge Fund and ERDF Objective Two funding to renovate the local market. The wider area is subject to economic regeneration with a new exhibition area in the Royal Docks.
Hyson Green and Forest Fields, Nottingham	Urban Task Force of late 1980s and early 1990s has been followed by the formation of a Nottingham Partnership Council which covers the two study areas as well as two other wards in the city. The Partnership Council distributes money obtained under the European Urban Programme within the city of Nottingham.

The experience of regeneration

Dingle, Liverpool	Has had an Estate Action scheme since 1994. An SRB Partnership area and one of the 11 'Pathways Partnerships' in Liverpool declared under European Objective One Region status, spending European Social Fund and European Regional Development Fund money. The Pathways Partnerships' main focus is on overcoming labour market exclusion.
Speke, Liverpool	Part of the Speke/Garston SRB Partnership. Speke is also one of the 11 'Pathways Partnerships' in Liverpool declared under European Objective One Region status, spending European Social Fund and European Regional Development Fund money.
St Hilda's, Middlesbrough	Physical and community development in 1980s using Housing Investment Programme and Urban Aid Grant funding. The St Hilda's Partnership was formed in 1993 with funding from the Teesside Training and Enterprise Council, Single Regeneration Budget Funding and Lottery funds. The Partnership has strategies in five areas, namely employment and training, youth and leisure, community crime prevention, housing and the environment, and heritage and tourism.
Norton Grange, Stockton-on-Tees	The estate is a major focus of the Stockton City Challenge funded since 1996. The work on the estate is overseen by a partnership including Stockton Borough Council, the Housing Corporation, four housing associations, DETR and a Community Forum. The complete revitalisation of the estate is progressed through strategies on crime, housing, the environment and employment.

that the residents were best placed to know what was needed locally and could avoid spending money on things which were not considered important by local people. This turned out to be an important issue, for, despite the arrangements for consultation and involvement, there was evidence that residents in some of the study areas did not think that the regeneration programmes were tackling their priorities. In St Hilda's in Middlesbrough, it was felt that there was insufficient priority being given to problems of crime and empty housing, and to youth needs. In Liverpool, there was a strong view that residents' opinions were neglected in the hype of regeneration, when what they wanted most were basic amenities like shops, street lighting and facilities for children.

There clearly were tensions about the degree of power afforded to communities over spending decisions. Mostly, communities were not in positions of power in regeneration, but the art of what is possible is shown by the Norton Grange Community Forum which had asserted its right to be involved in all regeneration decisions as an equal partner. However, in Liverpool, there were complaints that the community was not allowed sufficient say in how regeneration monies were to be spent. The community felt as if it was not really trusted by the authorities to spend the money wisely. In more than one neighbourhood,

Joined-up places?

interviewees were of the opinion that the residents' suggestions were not acted upon, there was no follow up to what they said, they could not identify things which had occurred because of their involvement, and their questions were not being answered. Yet, the case of the Nottingham Partnership illustrates the problems of going too far and involving residents in very lengthy and bureaucratic processes of making spending decisions (in this case of the distribution of Urban funds) with the result that attendance at Forum meetings had declined.

The communities' preference was to be asked early on what they wanted and then to be shown that their priorities were being acted upon. This requires flexibility so that communities do not receive answers which merely inform them that their priorities are outside the scope of the initiative; new solutions have to be found, even if this means spending money in new ways and being flexible about budget parameters.

The studies also highlighted problems associated with representative structures for community involvement in regeneration. In Nottingham, Middlesbrough and Stockton, people were suspicious of the representative structures designed to facilitate community involvement. Non-active residents and newer residents felt excluded from community forums which were said to be dominated by an active clique; there was little general knowledge about community representatives; and there was little experience of consultation by the representatives with the wider community. This indicates that hierarchical representative structures are insufficient to achieve community involvement in regeneration and that better resourcing and support for community representatives could help if they enabled more frequent canvassing of resident opinion to take place. Wider use of open meetings may also be appropriate if such meetings can be allied to key decision taking.

Communication and awareness of regeneration

In most of the cases studied, there was very limited knowledge about the non-housing aspects of local regeneration. Most people knew about physical changes in their area, or had some knowledge if the regeneration scheme had a focus, such as the Custom House in St Hilda's, Middlesbrough. But knowledge of what was being done in areas such as leisure, crime prevention, and training and employment was very patchy. In Liverpool, there was also widespread ignorance that the two neighbourhoods were in fact partnership areas.

Poor communication and poor awareness amongst the local population are a significant concern for a number of reasons. In the larger of the two London estates, Keir Hardie in Newham, poor communication meant that some residents were unsure of the boundaries of the regeneration area, and others were worried about unconfirmed rumours of demolitions in their street. Lack of information or misinformation may lie behind the scepticism, mistrust and frustration over regeneration which were felt by some residents in the study neighbourhoods. It cannot be a good thing if, as found in these studies, some people feel that the benefits of regeneration are not materialising locally, or that improvements are taking too long to have an effect. In contrast to those neighbourhoods, where vast physical change

The experience of regeneration

had taken place over a short period of time, in a couple of the neighbourhoods there was a view that nothing was changing yet housing and environmental improvements were needed:

People don't see any of the money that is being talked about. So you can't blame them for being disheartened. (Resident, Liverpool)

In general, the lack of visibility of much regeneration spending somehow has to be compensated for with good communication and information about the nature and timing of regeneration effects. Otherwise, a sceptical public will quickly become antagonistic to programmes that are often labelled a waste of money.

Is professional regeneration needed?

One has to recognise that there is a degree of scepticism and resentment of regeneration, which is seen as a professionalisation of the authorities' response to the needs of the community. In Liverpool, in particular, the interviewees saw dangers in the community becoming dependent on regeneration professionals. There was also resentment that such professionals, 'the suits of regeneration', were making 'vast sums' out of the community's needs without allowing the community to define their own requirements and whilst expecting a significant voluntary input from the community:

There are too many people in high places being paid vast amounts of money, expecting people to work voluntarily ... There are an awful lot of voluntary workers giving up their precious time, but they get nothing for it: no thanks, nothing. It's those at the top who get all the praise, and get paid £100,000 a year for doing nothing. (Resident, Liverpool)

The issue of the non-payment of community volunteers also surfaced in London:

There's a lot of money to be made out of poor people as long as you don't pay them to do it. (Resident, London)

There was a view in many quarters that regeneration was too focused on big projects and not enough on day-to-day matters. Regeneration was about 'grandiose ideas' whereas people wanted money to go into small, everyday things that people want. In a sense some of these communities were having change forced upon them through impressive regeneration schemes when what they wanted was basic, reliable, high quality public services with a local presence.

Some of the perceived deficiencies of the neighbourhoods raise questions about the isolation of the residents. In Trowbridge, Hackney, for example, a resident observed that expectations about local leisure facilities were unrealistic and unnecessary given the facilities in the borough as a whole. In Canning Town, where residents hear of planned leisure facilities in the northern part of the borough, the knowledge acts to deepen their sense of exclusion and heighten perceptions of being 'left out' again.

Divided by regeneration

In several instances, regeneration programmes had resulted in divisions within neighbourhoods. These divisions were not always

Joined-up places?

avoidable, but we should recognise that regeneration programmes that are phased over time, partial in their spatial coverage and involve diversification of tenure on predominantly council estates have the potential to exacerbate physical and social differences.

On the Trowbridge estate in Hackney, physical redevelopment in the 1990s had found the residents divided over the demolition of the 1960s' properties. The occupants of the tower blocks wanted the entire estate redeveloped but the older residents of the bungalows and low rise flats did not. In the end, both sides of this dispute, which involved active campaigns over regeneration, got some of what they wanted out of the redevelopment. But what was once one estate is now seen as two, with gates and a brick wall separating the two halves consisting of newer and older properties. The division is because of the bitterness left by the regeneration campaigns, but is also a generational divide (with older residents in the bungalows and young families in the newer houses) perpetuated by many factors including disputes about resources.

Divisions are less acute on the other London estate, Keir Hardie in Newham, but the fact that only some of the housing areas are marked for redevelopment is beginning to cause resentment, with forecasts of problems to come.

The physical regeneration of the Norton Grange estate in Stockton is largely positively received and is considered to have lifted the community's morale. It has, however, produced an estate of two halves, the council houses and the private and housing association houses; otherwise interpreted as newer and longer-term residents. Newer residents in the housing association properties were seen as 'outsiders' and they reported being subject to some harassment and intimidation from council house residents. The new part of the estate was looked on as self-contained.

Finally, in St Hilda's in Middlesbrough, the neighbourhood was widely seen to have been fragmented by the development of an area of private housing (called 'Tower Green'). Around 60 per cent of these houses were sold into owner occupation, but, in time, many of these have been sold on to private landlords. The other 40 per cent of the houses were sold to a housing association, but the properties became unpopular because of their small size, the rent levels, problems of harassment from other people on St Hilda's, as well as the fact that they acquired a poor reputation because of the kinds of tenants to whom they were let; though, what people referred to as 'druggies' and 'funny families' were not confined to the housing association properties but had appeared in the council stock as well. In this sense, the failure of the housing association development, which now lay entirely empty, was in part due to the failing reputation of the St Hilda's area as a whole. Most people, however, locate the start of this recent decline with the 1980s' redevelopment and the arrival of 'strangers' into the neighbourhood. This development of private and housing association housing was widely seen as 'disastrous' for the St Hilda's area, something it might not recover from.

Social regeneration: bringing the community together

In some of the neighbourhoods, social regeneration had yet to be achieved, and

The experience of regeneration

seemed to lag behind, rather than develop alongside, physical regeneration. Four issues in particular featured in the studies: parental responsibilities; community facilities; 'bringing the community together' (linked to community facilities); and housing management.

Social behaviour and social control

In Liverpool, young adults considered the two neighbourhoods to be in decline for social reasons. Observing the children of today, young adults were concerned that drug use was more widespread than in their childhoods and bad behaviour in general was worse at a younger age. They linked this to a lack of facilities for children.

On the Norton Grange estate in Stockton, there was a desire among the housing association tenants that the parents of both sets of houses, council and housing association, could come together as a community and agree some codes and standards of behaviour to address the problem of abuse from the children of council tenants. One optimistic resident said 'It's the people you've got to start working on not buildings'.

> *It would be nice if we could bond together and make the whole area into a good community and make sure that things that shouldn't happen don't happen.* (Housing association tenant, Norton Grange estate, Stockton-on-Tees)

> *When you're going off the rails, it would be identified and pointed out to your parents or, if somebody else was threatening you, then it would be sorted and dealt with there and then rather than today ... people tend not to want to get involved.* (Housing association tenant, Norton Grange estate, Stockton-on-Tees)

Similarly, on both London estates, an alleged lack of parenting skills was seen as an issue that divided the different generations, and the general lack of parental interest and control over their children's behaviour on the part of some residents caused problems for others.

Bringing the community together: community facilities and activities

On Norton Grange, people wanted adult engagement rather than non-involvement in social issues on the estate. They were concerned about the fact that Norton Grange is a multi-landlord estate, but wanted to see things through and create a community across the entire neighbourhood. The newer residents were to some degree frightened of the council tenants, felt the estate to be unfriendly, and did not like to go to the community centre, which is located on the council side of the estate. They regretted the lack of resources and organisation to try to bring the community together and integrate the various elements. In the London neighbourhoods, residents also recognised a need to bring together various sections of the community, and saw social activity, events and facilities as an appropriate means of doing so.

On the two London estates, there was concern about the effects of housing development upon the community and there were queries about whether the available facilities would keep pace with the expected influx of children into the neighbourhoods. Community divisions surfaced on the Trowbridge estate when residents were consulted about the siting of the planned community facilities. The preferred option for Wick residents was to locate them on the old part of Trowbridge estate; residents living there,

Joined-up places?

however, fearing disruption, wanted them opposite the estate, across the main road. Disappointment was expressed that plans for a new community complex did not include the necessary facilities to attract all sections of the community, including younger age groups. Some residents interviewed wanted a complex which catered for a wide range of groups and brought the community together. Both community halls and major community events were seen as necessary to achieve community cohesion:

> Until we have a place where everybody can meet, we don't have a community.
> (Resident, Trowbridge estate, London)

Housing management

Aspects of housing management were also seen to be potential contributors to social regeneration, notably housing allocations and tenancy management. On the Norton Grange estate in Stockton, both housing association and council tenants expressed the view that it was the council who had to improve their housing management, both to be as firm in dealing with anti-social behaviour as the associations, and by not permitting bad tenants to return to the estate:

> We are under stricter rules than in the council properties. They don't stand for any nonsense, which is a good thing. (Housing association tenant, Norton Grange estate, Stockton-on-Tees)

> The immediate future, well, if they don't get their fingers pulled out, I think the future looks bleak because, as I say, they said they were going to round up all the baddies – but they don't. Next thing you see they are back in again. So where do you go from there? (Council tenant, Norton Grange estate, Stockton-on-Tees)

Generally, clearer signals were given, and clearer undertakings from tenants extracted by the housing association landlords in a number of the study areas, and these were considered to be a good thing.

Two contrasting views emerged in different neighbourhoods about the contribution of housing association and co-operative allocations policies to social regeneration. On the one hand, there was the view that the non-profit sector was more careful about allocations and that this helps achieve cohesion and stability; thus, for example, the Wick Housing Co-operative residents themselves vet allocations to beneficial effect. On the other hand, in Dingle, Liverpool, and as we have seen in St Hilda's, Middlesbrough, the housing associations are largely blamed for 'putting anybody in' and in so doing giving the neighbourhood more problems to cope with.

Housing allocations were also seen as reinforcing the divisions on the Trowbridge estate in London. The former tower block dwellers were given priority in the allocation of new houses. They tended to live next door to one another thus making the integration of newcomers more difficult. The main allocations issue on the London estates, however, concerned a perceived lack of priority for locals. Such priority was desired for two reasons. First, to give the next generation a stake in the neighbourhood. The parents of young people felt that their sons and daughters deserved to have a choice of staying in the area when they formed their own households:

The experience of regeneration

Youngsters have to be given the choice of staying here. Then the community spirit will continue. Now it's deteriorating fast.
(Resident, Keir Hardie estate, London)

Second, priority was desired for other close relatives of residents:

The council say it's not equal opportunities policy to move people who know each other into the area. Yet it's rubbish if your mother needs you. It's not racism, it's just not fair. And this is a black person telling you.
(Resident, Keir Hardie estate, London)

In both cases, it was expected that a change in policy would impact on intergenerational continuity on the estates.

(Re)generating optimism and the need for jobs

Clearly, an important aspect of the revitalisation of communities is to give them back hope for the future, but the study areas varied in the degree of optimism generated by the regeneration programmes.

Physical improvements, the enhancement of housing and the environment were an important means of instilling optimism in communities. This was especially the case on the Norton Grange estate in Stockton, where extensive physical change had taken place recently. As a result, people felt better about the estate and some had hope for the future whilst recognising that the high levels of unemployment had yet to be tackled. Similarly, residents on the Trowbridge estate in London, which had also had extensive recent redevelopment, were among the most optimistic found in the studies.

But this optimism was also linked to knowledge of economic regeneration in the wider local area which residents were hopeful that they or their children would share in; it seems that awareness of wider change combined with a good feeling about one's local neighbourhood because of recent changes brought about a feeling of optimism among residents that opportunities would arise to which they would have access.

Physical change was important for community morale, but also because of its effects on a neighbourhood's image in the wider urban area, and both of these were linked to employment prospects according to the beliefs and attitudes of residents. Young people in Dingle and Speke in Liverpool identified the poor physical environment of their neighbourhoods as a primary cause of the negative image held of themselves and their home areas. Moreover, they believed that the bad reputation of their neighbourhoods and fellow residents would count against them in the market for the limited employment opportunities available in their parts of the city of Liverpool.

Where physical regeneration had gone wrong, and/or where empty houses started to reappear in noticeable numbers, the residents were pessimistic that the image of their neighbourhood would change sufficiently to offer them a better future. This was the case in St Hilda's, Middlesbrough, where there was widespread pessimism about the future. The despondency was of a fundamental nature, i.e. that the neighbourhood would not survive and would be 'closed down' as unviable.

Jobs were a major concern in all the study areas. Where attempts were known to be made to attract new jobs into the nearby or surrounding area, residents in Newham and

Joined-up places?

Nottingham were cautious or realistic about the prospects for local employment gain. There was an awareness that such jobs could go to others in the city, that such jobs might not last, and that the people from their neighbourhoods still lack many of the skills sought. But, in Liverpool, one found pessimism both about the creation of new jobs and about the likelihood of local people getting those jobs. There was already anger that many general labouring jobs created through the regeneration programmes went to people from other cities, never mind local residents from the neighbourhoods in question. As well as jobs for adults, residents in Liverpool identified a need for 'little jobs' for older schoolchildren to give them some financial independence.

Jobs were seen as the key to regeneration by many interviewees. There was a belief that many local problems would be solved if more people had jobs. For many young people in Dingle and Speke, their main desire was that they would have realistic employment opportunities in the future. The end result from jobs, in their eyes, would be happy, decent people. Their objectives were social as well as economic:

> *I just want to get a good job really and just be happy. I don't want to be on the dole.*
> (Young resident, Dingle, Liverpool)

> *Give people more jobs. Yeah, get more jobs for people in the area. People would all be decent then.* (Young resident, Speke, Liverpool)

Similarly, the London study indicated that unemployment was associated with an underground economy and drug dealing, the effects of which were to undermine social cohesion by leading residents in such areas to 'keep themselves to themselves'.

The litmus test of social regeneration and community optimism would be that people wanted to stay in the neighbourhoods and expected others to want to join them. However, whilst active and longer-established residents clearly wanted to remain in these neighbourhoods, there was no consensus on staying among newer residents. It rather depended whether they had themselves become active locally, or saw a real prospect of social integration with the longer-established residents.

Regeneration through partnership working

Finally, the neighbourhood studies, in particular the Nottingham study, highlighted several issues surrounding partnership working which make this a very difficult method of implementing change, both for residents and for officials. There are institutional, structural and cultural obstacles to overcome for multisectoral regeneration partnerships to operate successfully.

Institutionally, the problems surround the need to clarify the remit and objectives of the partnership. A local partnership can be formed for one or more of many purposes and it is important to know which of these are relevant from the start and whether others are to be possibilities further down the track. A local partnership might have a number of purposes including being a consultative body; a body that identifies and prioritises needs for the local area; a regulatory body for local public services, which monitors services and handles complaints; a decision-making body with delegated authority to commit public agencies

The experience of regeneration

to courses of action or to itself spend a delegated budget allocated by several agencies (this is the model about which much disappointment and scepticism were found in some of the study areas); or a service provider in its own right. Difficulties arise if the original remit is not made clear in terms of what powers and responsibilities are available and that are not available, and, then, if the partners have very different views as to the best model to adopt or work for.

The institutional environment is one of a plethora of potential public, private, voluntary and community sector partners who all have different powers, responsibilities, expertise and knowledge of the issues. Another important aspect of the institutional environment that was identified as problematic for local regeneration partnerships was the fact that both the local authority and other public agencies are involved in several partnerships at once in a competitive funding regime. This meant that alliance and commitments were likely to fluctuate in strength or shift altogether as centrally determined opportunities or priorities change. Clear commitments of a sustainable nature are required from partners in such circumstances.

The structural issues facing local partnerships stem from the departmental nature of local government and the party-political nature of local politics. Local area-based policy making of the holistic, joined-up kind being sought by the government, which involves negotiated power sharing at the local level is very difficult if local government wishes to conduct policy making on a departmental basis. As we have seen in the studies, though, decentralised structures (if decentralisation includes policy making and delegated budgets) can help here. Similarly, policy making by local partnerships may cause conflict with local councillors elected on a political party manifesto if the principles or preferred policies of the local partnership are at odds either with those of the local councillor or of the controlling party of the council.

The cultural challenge of local partnership working faces both residents and officials. Residents may have to drop a predilection for adversarial relations with public bodies and adapt to negotiation and bargaining as a way of working. But residents can also expect partnerships to be discursive, inclusive and collaborative, generating trust among partners. The latter will in turn require public officials to move away from a legalistic, bureaucratic and hierarchical method of operation with little consultation or delegation. The conduct of business in an open manner, with flexibility in decision making and the maintenance of trust, will be crucial to the endurance of partnerships with local people. The Nottingham study found evidence of mistrust of the other partners on the part of the local communities, with little expectation that the local authority will delegate power and authority. This seemed well-founded given other evidence to suggest that councillors and officials have reservations in principle and in practice about the idea of giving away properly acquired responsibilities to lay people with insufficient competence.

The experience of regeneration: conclusion

Despite the recognised need and desire for change in the study neighbourhoods, there was a significant amount of scepticism, and in some cases cynicism, about regeneration. Regeneration was seen as a professionalisation of the neighbourhoods' problems; a process in which the residents themselves were not afforded control; for all the talk, the community was not trusted, though it was consulted. Residents wanted to be in the 'driving seat' of regeneration, where they themselves decided what was to be done, set the priorities and received appropriate feedback to inform them when and how their requirements were to be met. There was a feeling that the professionals were 'on top, not on tap'.

Formal representative structures within regeneration programmes, in the main, did not seem to have worked well. Too many people felt disenfranchised by such structures, either because there was insufficient contact between the residents and the community representatives, or the representatives were felt to be unrepresentative, or because the views of the community became 'lost' in the administrative mechanisms of the public bodies concerned, with little response or feedback given on community views. Residents were in many cases ignorant of the range of activities being undertaken as part of regeneration, unsure of the timings involved and unconvinced about the outcomes to be expected. It was clear that, as regeneration had extended beyond visible, physical change, communication on these key aspects had not adapted and resident awareness was poorer.

The content of what was being done for these neighbourhoods came under question, especially as conceived under the label 'regeneration'. In several cases, there were doubts that regeneration programmes were meeting resident priorities; indeed, it was not clear whether such priorities had ever been systematically identified. Although large-scale physical change was often required in the study neighbourhoods, there was also a strong view that regeneration was an approach full of 'grandiose ideas' and hyperbole, when what people most wanted (apart from jobs) were small-scale local amenities and decent public services with a local presence for a variety of groups within the community. Issues of basic public services to these areas featured as much, if not more, than the need for large-scale projects and change. Residents wanted local authorities and other public bodies to perform better for them; they did not want to have to try doing the job for such bodies.

The studies demonstrated a set of linkages between physical change, social regeneration and jobs. Social regeneration was not keeping pace with physical change in many cases. New forms of community development and new protocols for housing management were required for this. Physical change was an essential prerequisite for boosting community morale and shifting the negative image of neighbourhoods which had labour market spillovers. In turn, jobs were seen as an important part of the solution to many social problems in poor neighbourhoods. But community optimism depended on a combination of significant housing and environmental improvements within the neighbourhood and economic development in the surrounding urban area which the residents felt could offer them opportunities. Regeneration to date had been predominantly inward-looking and not outward-looking enough to tackle the social and economic isolation of the neighbourhoods, or their negative image and reputation.

5 Conclusions

Social cohesion

The first basic question this research has addressed is 'Do poor neighbourhoods lack social cohesion?' The answer has to be 'No, they do not'. The studies provide substantial evidence of active social networks of mutual aid and strong bonds of trust and familiarity in disadvantaged areas. In that sense, it would be wrong to characterise many such neighbourhoods as disorganised and lacking cohesion. But, as we have stressed, cohesion comes in many different forms and may have negative as well as positive features, and can be conflictual rather than unifying. Cohesion can be inward-looking and the product of adversity. There are bonds of reciprocity and feelings of attachment, local commitment and resilience in the face of adversity, decline and disillusionment. Many of the residents of disadvantaged neighbourhoods do not lack enthusiasm, commitment and energy. These are areas where people have had to adapt to a hostile world where regeneration activity is swimming against a tide of entrenched unemployment and underemployment, and retail and commercial disinvestment. These adaptations may in some cases be individual and perverse but they are nonetheless attempts to make things work despite the odds.

Having said that our study areas exhibit notable elements of social cohesion, we must also recognise that, in adverse circumstances, not everything is sweetness and light. The social cohesion of these areas is often fractured or disjointed. Disadvantaged neighbourhoods display many of the tensions of contemporary life in acute forms, between young and old, families and no-child households, haves (relatively speaking) and have-nots. These tensions are exacerbated by the density of use of the neighbourhood by different groups with nowhere else to go, by the need to fight and squabble over scarce resources and by the sheer difficulties of 'getting by'. On a national scale, there may be a need to 'Bring Britain together' but, on a local scale there is also a need within disadvantaged areas to bring communities together within their shared space – the neighbourhood. Thus, community spirit and local commitment among elements of the local populace are not the same thing as social cohesion in a rounded sense, and there is a need for community development, not simply community participation in initiatives.

Social regeneration is an agenda that has to be taken seriously as part of renewal initiatives. This requires first and foremost a thorough understanding of the history, structure and social relations of an area so that the origins of present-day divisions (some created or reinforced by past regeneration initiatives), images and reputations can be identified and appropriate ways forward developed. The main task in many disadvantaged neighbourhoods is to bring the community together by building links between constituent groups. Building social cohesion within communities which are experiencing social tensions involves enabling communities to derive shared values and codes of conduct for themselves. On these issues, regeneration programmes can work with, rather than deliver to, communities, but such work has to appear to be non-patronising. Conducting regeneration through more open, communicative means than the use of representative structures may also help in this developmental task.

Joined-up places?

The provision of adequate community facilities, clubs and activities, some run by the user groups rather than for them, are important enabling mechanisms for cohesion, but, in several areas, residents commented on the lack of such opportunities for interaction. Finally, the housing management function is seen as both a culprit and part of the solution to social regeneration issues. The relevant aspects of housing management include considering how social housing allocation policies can be adapted to contribute to social cohesion, residential stability and community development within disadvantaged neighbourhoods. Speedy repair and reletting systems were seen as essential to maintaining community morale (see below) and firm tenancy management, put in place with the community's support, was frequently desired. Social regeneration concerns how to bridge the gaps between resident groups in disadvantaged neighbourhoods; how to make the most of the social capital which already exists within such areas; and how to ensure that all who want it can develop a stake in the future of the area and in the well-being of everyone who lives there, and be provided with means to express this.

The neighbourhood

We also asked 'Do neighbourhoods still matter?' Once again, the answer is a firm 'Yes'. The research has shown how the physical and social aspects of the community and the neighbourhood are intertwined. Decline in the physical environment, especially if this involved the loss or dereliction of a neighbourhood's historic and landmark buildings, had a deleterious impact on a community's view of itself and a psycho-social impact on residents' well-being, and, in the residents' eyes, this was a major factor influencing other people's view of the area and its people. Physical improvements were essential to boost the morale of disadvantaged communities and a prerequisite for changing an area's external image. Local community action to improve the environment was shown to be a route towards community development. Moreover, small but visible projects can have a disproportionate impact on creating a mood of optimism and on generating a feeling that the area has a future.

The research highlighted two retreats of some concern. First, a perceived shift from programmes of physical regeneration towards programmes focused mainly on developing social and human capital. In most disadvantaged areas, both approaches are necessary. Poor communities need physical change in a real and a psychological sense. One challenge for regeneration programmes based on the longer-term development of training and skills is that communities want to 'see things happening', which presents a formidable communication problem for regeneration.

Second, there was evidence of the retreat of public services from disadvantaged areas. Neighbourhoods had experienced the loss or scaling down of the local public service presence from the local authority and from other statutory services and public bodies. This was part of the keen sense of loss and narrowing of neighbourhood function felt by residents. But the loss of local public services is important for other reasons. Such closures and retreats simply made life more difficult for people with few resources and many needs. A lack of a local public and statutory presence contributed to problems of social control, more

Conclusions

crime and social retreat by vulnerable residents. In such circumstances, communities inferred that their areas did not have a future without a visible local public commitment. More than this, the needs of such areas required not only locally delivered public services, but such services had to have local flexibility of budgets and policies. It is not so much that national policies have to improve (as stated by the Prime Minister) but that more local and less national policies are needed.

Urban regeneration

A third major strand of the studies was to assess the residents' views of the impact of past regeneration initiatives. It has to be said that there was a great deal of scepticism and cynicism about regeneration programmes. The professionalisation of regeneration had highlighted the contrast between highly paid implementers of regeneration and the unpaid input to regeneration by local residents. There is clearly a difficulty in creating a culture of partnership in a political environment which is heavily managed by outsiders. There is an important ethical issue about voluntarism in regeneration, namely should community participants be paid a decent wage for their work? Regeneration programmes were not seen as contributing to local employment and the economy in ways in which they could.

Consultation structures in regeneration programmes appeared to lack feedback-loops through which communities could be informed as to the actions taken on their suggestions and priorities. On too many occasions, residents were of the view that their opinions had not counted and that nothing had been done about their suggestions. This may or may not be true. What is significant is that this was so often felt to be the case. But the resentment felt about regeneration reveals an ambiguity on the part of residents, stemming from the basics not being right. On the one hand, residents recognise the need for vast physical changes in many areas, but, on the other hand, they also feel that regeneration is all about hype and grandiose ideas. What people feel they really need are decent public services with a local face. In their eyes, the small things were being missed for the big visions.

Neighbourhoods in an urban context

On the larger scale, disadvantaged neighbourhoods suffer disconnection from their towns and cities. Feelings of isolation in deprived areas are acute. These are 'far away' places in both the residents' minds and the minds of other city dwellers. Even where change had taken place, that reality had not been successfully conveyed to the wider populace. In order to overcome stigma and a poor image, disadvantaged areas have to become 'permeable places'. Transport services and social opportunities have to help expand the worlds of the residents of such areas, and people from other areas have to be given reasons to go to these places. The lack of interaction with other city residents was recognised by people in poor areas. The research did not uncover much evidence of 'outward-looking' regeneration programmes.

Such places have been characterised as 'neighbourhoods that don't work' (Social Exclusion Unit, 1998). We have seen that this is not an accurate social description, but it is literally true in terms of employment and is at

Joined-up places?

the heart of the problem. The point about neighbourhood integration into the urban arena is also relevant to employment goals. Residents were clear that jobs are needed to regenerate neighbourhoods both economically and socially. Optimism among the community, where it was found, rested on the knowledge that economic development in surrounding parts of the urban area would provide opportunities for the employment of unemployed adults and young people. Joblessness was considered to lie at the root of many social problems, so that economic development would bring social as well as economic gains. There was, however, also a great deal of pessimism about the prospects of people from disadvantaged areas obtaining jobs in key urban developments.

Joined-up places

In summary, we can say that disadvantaged neighbourhoods have to be considered and developed as 'joined-up places' in several respects. First, communities within disadvantaged neighbourhoods need opportunities to be brought together, and social development which gives everyone a stake in the area and which forms common values, aspirations and codes of conduct is desirable. Second, disadvantaged areas need public services and regeneration initiatives which can respond locally and flexibly to the interconnectedness of their problems. Third, the physical and social isolation of many disadvantaged areas within their host towns and cities has to be tackled in a concerted manner, not left as a potential by-product of other changes. Fourth, there is a need for explicit linkage between regeneration initiatives for specific areas within cities and citywide policies of social, economic and political development, so that the contribution of the latter to the former can be planned.

References

Andersen, H., Munck, R., Fagan, C., Goldson, B., Hall, D., Lansley, J., Novak, T., Melville, R., Moore, R. and Ben-Tovim, G. (1999) *Neighbourhood Images in Liverpool: 'It's All Down To the People'*. York: JRF

Bartley, B. (1998) 'Exclusion, invisibility and the neighbourhood in West Dublin', in G. Cars, A. Madinopour, and J. Allen (eds) *Social Exclusion in European Cities*. London: Jessica Kingsley, pp 131–56

Baumgartner, M. (1988) *The Moral Order of the Suburbs*. Oxford: Oxford University Press

Brower, S. (1996) *Good Neighbourhoods*. Westport, CT and London: Praeger

Cars, G., Madinopour, A. and Allen, J. (eds) (1998) *Social Exclusion in European Cities*. London: Jessica Kingsley

Cattell, V. and Evans, M. (1999) *Neighbourhood Images in East London: Social Capital and Social Networks on Two East London Estates*. York: JRF

Ellen, I.G. and Turner, M.A. (1997) 'Does neighbourhood matter? Assessing recent evidence', *Housing Policy Debate*, Vol. 8, issue 4, pp. 833–66

European Commission (1996) *First Report on Economic and Social Cohesion*. Luxembourg: Office for the Official Publications of the European Communities

Healey, P. (1998) 'Institutionalist theory, social exclusion and governance', in G. Cars, A. Madinopour and J. Allen (eds) *Social Exclusion in European Cities*. London: Jessica Kingsley

Henning, C. and Lieberg, M. (1996) 'Strong ties or weak ties? Neighbourhood networks in a new perspective', *Scandinavian Housing and Planning Research*, Vol. 13, pp. 3–26

Hirschfield, A. and Bowers, K. (1997) 'The effect of social cohesion on levels of recorded crime in disadvantaged areas', *Urban Studies*, Vol. 34, pp. 1275–95

Kasarda, J. and Janowitz, M. (1974) 'Community attachment in mass society', *American Sociological Review*, Vol. 39, pp. 328–39

Kearns, A. and Forrest, R. (1999) *Social Cohesion, Neighbourhoods and Cities* (forthcoming)

McCulloch, A. (1997) 'You've fucked up the estate and now you're carrying a briefcase', in P. Hoggett (ed.) *Contested Communities*. Bristol: Policy Press

Portes, A. and Landolt, P. (1996) 'The downside of social capital', *American Prospect*, Summer, pp. 18–21

Putnam, R. (1993) 'The prosperous community: social capital and economic growth', *American Prospect*, Spring, pp. 35–42

Putnam, R. (1996) 'The strange disappearance of civic America', *American Prospect*, Winter, pp. 34–48

Putnam, R. (1998) 'Foreword', *Housing Policy Debate*, Vol. 9, p. 1

Sampson, R. (1988) 'Local friendship ties and community attachment in mass society', *American Sociological Review*, Vol. 53, pp. 766–79

Silburn, R., Lucas, D., Page, R. and Hanna, L. (1999) *Neighbourhood Images in Nottingham: Social Cohesion and Neighbourhood Change*. York: JRF

Social Exclusion Unit (1998) *Bringing Britain Together: A National Strategy for Neighbourhood Renewal*, Cm. 4045. London: HMSO

Suttles, G. (1972) *The Social Construction of Communities*. Chicago: University of Chicago Press

Wood, M. and Vamplew, C. (1999) *Neighbourhood Images in Teesside: Regeneration or Decline?* York: JRF